CONTINUITY OF LIFE · VOLUME 3

Transition and Survival Technologies

Interdimensional Consciousness as Healing, Survival and Beyond

Written and Illustrated by Dr. Angela deAngelis

Continuity of Life Series

Volume 1

Endings Are Beginnings:
Navigating Your Hard Times into Higher States

Volume 2

Embracing Eternity:
The Life Force Does Not Die

Volume 3

Transition and Survival Technologies:
Interdimensional Consciousness as Healing, Survival and Beyond

Volume 4

Healing Earth in All Her Dimensions:
Personal, Species and Planetary Healing Tools

Transition and Survival Technologies

Interdimensional Consciousness as Healing, Survival and Beyond

Written and Illustrated by
Dr. Angela deAngelis

Light Technology Publishing

ISBN 1-891824-68-6
EAN 978-1-891824-68-5

Published & Printed by

Light Technology PUBLISHING
www.lighttechnology.com

800-450-0985

PO Box 3540
Flagstaff, AZ 86003
publishing@lighttechnology.net

Contents

List of Figures

Author's Note

Thank you for visiting these pages. Our paths will touch as this book forms a doorway into the continuity of life, into the core persona of our essences. Here the continuity of life grabs hold, makes its reality loud and clear. Here the life force makes its ongoing, ever-healing, ever-evolving, ever-present, streaming essence known. Here the precious resource, the consciousness, lives on.

This book, *Transition and Survival Technologies: Interdimensional Conciousness as Healing, Survival and Beyond*, is Volume Three of this four-volume *Continuity of Life* series. This third volume builds upon the material presented in the previous two volumes to now take readers further on their inner as well as their interdimensional journeys into the world of the ever-evolving and expanding human consciousness.

The material in these *Continuity of Life* volumes is written for a broad range of readers. No particular belief system of any spiritual, scientific, philosophical or religious nature is required. Whether one does or does not believe in a higher power or God or gods of some form, is an atheist or holds something other than these identities, there is a journey here, a journey in which we can examine our consciousnesses for their limits, for the possibility that:

- The limits of our consciousnesses are beyond what we may presently think of these as being.
- Our consciousnesses can have some say in their own

evolution and in the evolution of all human consciousness.

- Human consciousness is not at all complete in its evolution.

This *Continuity of Life* series does not insist that a reader has to believe in life after death—or even in soul, for that matter. Instead, this material offers the possibility that humans are able to develop and actually have been developing their consciousnesses to a point far past what they may think are their limitations—to a point where these consciousnesses might even be able to override emotional and physical conditions, to exist and to survive independent of physical conditions and physical bodies themselves. Again, this thinking—the strengthening and expansion of the human consciousness—is intended to serve all readers regardless of their own worldviews.

So, readers, play with these ideas, see where you choose to go with them, take them in the way you wish to, or simply, if you prefer, be entertained by them. In fact, readers are encouraged to view this material as any or all of the following:

- food for thought
- fuel for imagination
- fiction or fantasy
- metaphor for self-discovery
- exploration of concepts regarding reality
- stimulation of psychological or scientific inquiry
- spiritual inspiration
- a bridge between one's own and others' schools of thought
- a piece of the inner journey

- fuel for evolution
- something other than the above

However a reader chooses to frame her or his intake of the material in this book, certain care should be taken. The metaphors, exercises and teachings in this volume must be practiced with a commitment to use them carefully and never to impose them on others. When applying or teaching this material, do so only in circumstances of the highest intent and the right use of free will. Whether applying this knowledge to "in life" challenges or to physical death, know that this knowledge, if abused, may harm its abuser and others. Never use this knowledge against your own or others' free wills. When applying this knowledge to psychological and physical transitions, healings and even physical deaths, remember that the ability to undergo transition of any sort, including to die well and to die at will, is ours, and the respect and consciousness to apply this ability—*only under correct circumstances*—is also ours.

Your understanding of the concepts herein will evolve as you consider and reconsider them. Since these concepts are so very important, so very profound, much of what is being taught here is written between the lines. Much of the focus herein is upon the fundamental elements of healing and transition—the movement of consciousness from one state to another, from phase to phase of "transitional travel" through the steps in consciousness that build toward conscious shifts (LEAPs) to whole new perceptions and thus whole new realities of mind, of existences.

We can consciously bring about effective transformative shifts during each and every one of our "in daily life" and "end of life" changes, recoveries, healings, transitions and deaths. We can engage in this process of *conscious shift construction* each step of the way, every day. It is all in how we live our lives, what we see and know while we live. We can indeed practice conscious shift construction—practice and prepare for what may appear (from the standpoint offered by a physical lifetime) to be the ultimate death, physical death—and in this very preparation, realize that physical death is not an ultimate death but rather can be another step along the way, because . . .

THE LIFE FORCE DOES NOT DIE.
THE HIGHER PERSONA NEED NOT DIE.
THE CONSCIOUSNESS CAN LIVE ON.
THE HUMAN CONSCIOUSNESS CAN HAVE A SAY IN ITS EVOLUTION.

This knowledge is our birthright and it is for us to use, to understand, to maximize and to carry with us into the next level of our existence as we evolve and survive . . . as we captain the evolution of human consciousness to newer, higher states.

The Eternal Journey

Wander on.
Realms, new realities,
having been here all along,
await.
Such a grand undertaking,
seeing this lifetime . . .
seeing this reality
as something the self can see as it wishes.
Yet such a step it is along the epic journey,
the quintessential pilgrimage,
the honoring of self.
Crystalline windows,
clearer than clear,
pure vision beyond all seeing,
rush of sensations beyond
the material plane.
Consciousness,
consciousness,
crystals of consciousness,
forming and unforming,
becoming more than they are,
more than they have known themselves to be,
more than here and now.
Consciousness reaching beyond its fading limits
because **IT CAN.**

— Angela deAngelis

AN OPENING LIGHT

BASIC LIGHT-ENERGY-ACTION-PROCESS STEPS

LEAP Level	LEAP Type	Volume of *Continuity of Life* Series This Is Discussed In
Seeing Cycles	Ground Level of LEAPs	Volume One
One	Embracing	Volume Two
Two	Quickening	Volume Two
Three	Willing the Exit	Volume Two
Four	Leaping to the Next Dimension	Volume Three
Five	Ascending	Volume Three
Six	Catharting Beyond	Volume Three
Seven	Metascending to a New Niche	Volume Four
Eight	Achieving Metastasis and High Metaxis	Volume Four

PART I

How to Get Out of an Existing Emotional or Physical Condition or Reality

Part I of this book explores the notion—as fantasy, as metaphor and as distinct possibility—of "getting out" of psychological and physical conditions, such as problem patterns and "dis-eases," as well as the physical plane itself (including the physical body and the physical reality). While so doing, the consciousness can see itself as surviving the exit and moving beyond old patterns and realities. The following chapters invite readers on a creative dreamlike journey into ideas, offering a way to consider possibilities . . . as adventures. The immense relevance to daily life, including mental and physical health, is in the ongoing, even daily opportunities for the exercise and development of the consciousness.

Chapter 1

Leaving the Body

Now Cassim had forgotten the magic word. He had had his mind on the gold. The more he tried to think of the magic word, the more frightened he became. . . . The gold was no good to him if he couldn't get out of the cave.

—*"Ali Baba and the Forty Thieves,"*
1001 NIGHTS

When you have willed your exit from your old daily patterns, old habits and addictions, perhaps even from the flesh of your present life, there begins a great adventure in healing, transition and the death of old mindsets. Now you can discover for yourself what it means to transition to new realities, to die and survive—what it means to have a say in the course and nature of your daily life, of your health, of your physical transitions and of your deaths.

Death Is a Metaphor

All death is a metaphor for transition. Let's stop right here and dispel any confusion about "metaphor." Generally speaking, metaphor is the application of a word or phrase to an idea,

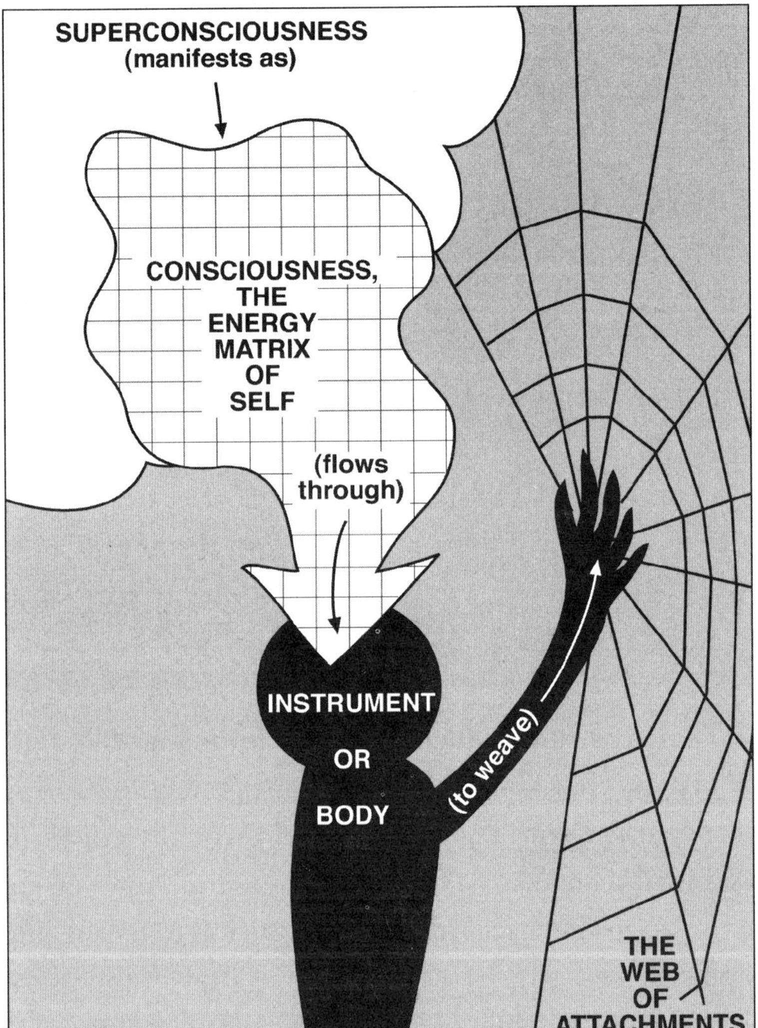

Figure 1.1. Consciousness matrix flows through.

sensation or thing, for purposes of comparison, with the goal of increasing understanding of this idea, sensation or thing. However, metaphor is being used here as this, plus so much more than this.

Metaphor is a tool for allowing the mind to explore new possibilities, new ways of understanding things. Metaphor is a playground for the mind, a place to explore aspects of reality not readily seen directly. Metaphor creates a place in the mind for the mind to examine its reality and its ways of knowing about reality.

The metaphors applied herein assist us to master understanding of death, even of physical death, and to master life's challenges, cycles and changes. Metaphors are tools that can help ease out of resistance to change. The tendency to resist change of any sort is natural. For example, even after getting out of your present phase of life (or perhaps even your physical body), you might be tempted to cling to it.

You may cling to your emotional or physical reality, even to your physical body, as if you need it to survive. This is natural. You have needed your physical body to survive physically. Yet there comes a time when it is necessary to leave the body to save the wealth of spirit, the riches of what you might call soul—let's call this "soul" thing *consciousness* here—that you have acquired while in that body. Even if you understand this and exit your reality (your body), your own and sometimes others' emotional bodies may not want to let you—or what is thought of as being you—go.

It therefore pays to further examine this getting out (of a dying stage of life or of a physical body). It matters not which transition you presently face, as you are always undergoing one and you are always, every day, presented with opportunities for practicing and mastering transition and death. Hence, the metaphor for all change being a form of transition or death of old patterns is most valuable. In "death as a metaphor" is the key to survival through expansion of the self.

Embrace the Unknown

The deep desire to move forward into reality-shifting arises when there is a deep "survival type" drive to do so. Quite often this desire—or its actual purpose—remains subconscious. It pays to pull this desire into the consciousness so that it can be clearly understood and not misinterpreted.

There comes a time when there is nothing to do but leave the old life, the old emotional or even physical reality, and eventually even the old physical body and the emotional body it has generated. You know this juncture when you come to it, although you may, in some subtle (or overt) way, try not to see it, try not to recognize that you are there. At this juncture, you might find yourself resistant to dying, perhaps nostalgic for the past, even if it is an outgrown troubled past. You may want to hang on to the familiar. Even if you have released all or most of your attachments to the familiar (as discussed in Volume Two), you might still prefer the familiar to the unknown. Of course, preference itself is a form of attachment.

This preference is often found even among those who have endured much emotional and/or physical suffering. To a point, known pain might appear safer or more comfortable than unknown—or feared—pain, whether or not pain is truly part of the equation. In fact, pain may be more a part of fear of letting go than fear of the transition itself. Death itself—the transition (of pattern and of body) death—need not hurt and actually does not hurt. The pain some associate with change, even with physical death, is most likely:

- the pain of attachment to physicality
- the pain of withdrawal from that attachment or addiction to that reality.
- the pain of not being able to fully recognize and enhance what is taking place in the physical dimension by understanding it

Recognize the Desire to Hang On to the Familiar

It is important to recognize the difference between: (1) hanging on to what is familiar, and (2) moving forward into reality-shifting, itself a form of death. These are *two different drives*, although frequently commingled and confused.

The desire to hang on to the familiar can camouflage itself as what might feel to be the *survival instinct*, the misinterpretation of which can even lead a person to remain in a sick body, a sick relationship or an ailing or dying system longer than he or she has to. Sometimes the individual experiencing this confusion remains resistant to transitioning—to the shifting of realities, to the dying out of one and into a new life—far too long. Her or his spirit loses energy and begins to die.

This excessive wearing down and waning of the spirit, the consciousness, is not the death to seek. This is the conscious-depleting death transition to avoid by *consciously* undergoing physical and emotional transitions and death releases in order to preserve, even maximize, the energy of the spirit, the maximum essence of the consciousness.

Sometimes moving forward into a reality-shifting phase feels like dying. However, "dying" is just a word for transitioning. While resisting change (acting out the above-explained desire to hang on to the familiar), desiring to hang on to the familiar is one way of dealing with the need for or actual eventuality of a shift in one's reality.

Spilling into this shift, unknowingly or knowingly, can feel like swimming in a sea whose tide and direction is unclear. Consciously moving forward into this phase is highly preferable, as this allows the conscious navigation of transition and even death.

Leave a Dying System as Consciously as Possible

So often the desire to cling to the familiar is actually dangerous. We may miss cues and indications that *change is necessary to survive.* We have all heard the story of those who will not leave a sinking ship. *It is of tantamount importance that you leave a dying system before it wears you down or even takes you down with it.* This can be a matter of energy preservation. At a certain point, the energy you expend to hang on to the familiar is energy much needed to maintain and enhance your consciousness.

Get out while you can still get out whole and fully alive! This dictum is not so readily embraced or appreciated by a heavily corded and troubled person. Until you see the truth about survival, that survival means transitioning when it is time, you are living a sort of lie:

THE LIE IS THAT THIS REALITY IS ALL THERE IS.

This reality is what you make it, and you *can* learn to expand your reality. Your consciousness is yours to work with. You can let it live in ways that you may have been told (or may have somehow come to believe) you cannot. Too often one feels as if only a particular religious orientation can see things this way, and that, if not part of this orientation, the thinking is out of line. However, whether or not you believe in a particular definition of a god, in a god at all, or in heaven or an afterlife—whether or not you are an atheist or deist or God-minded person—you *can* develop your consciousness. You *can* maximize your consciousness beyond where you are and beyond where many of you have been told you must be.

Once you allow yourself to see the truth, to realize the need for shedding your reality (your body or behavior or relationship or system), you must *let yourself out of your illusion*, let your lie out of your system or skin. Here you might find others putting up strong resistance to your leaving. (Many people will not want you to change, to shift realities, to die.) Just as you may cling to the familiar, the people around you might not want you to change away from what is familiar. *Learn to recognize the sensation of your own and others' clinging to your or their reality and wanting you to stay within it.* It is good to know what this is, to be able to recognize this when it is taking place.

Clear the Runway

Remember that physical death is a model of all change and transition. Recall from Volume One that there are going to be three basic stages of your death out of this physical life: basic physical death, then emotional death, then mental death. Physical death is quite frequently perceived as more challenging than emotional death. But note again that, odd as it may seem, the presumed pain of physical death is actually more emotional than physical. A troubling physical sensation must be registered as such for it be *felt* to be troubling. (Ideally, physical sensations that can send important notices that something must be attended to can be registered without the suffering and pain oft involved in calling the attention to it. Pain is a signal that can likely be read in other ways if understood as such.)

It is the entanglement of the emotional body with the physical that can render any sort of change or death emotionally and physically challenging. Again, what makes leaving the body or reality seem so difficult is:

- fear of the unknown
- resistance to shifting to a new reality
- matters of managing any pain entangled with this fear and/or resistance
- general lack of preparation for death

Many pain management problems can be tied to emotional-body entanglement. This is a complex topic that will be further explored in future volumes.

Look Ahead

Before you die, generate for yourself your own personal picture of where you want to go after your transition or death—a clear definition of the beyond you want to think of finding there. This picture is yours to generate. Use your imagination—this is all right. Create a reality you want to believe in. Clarify and further detail this reality for yourself according to your own worldviews (or use a sacred teaching if you prefer).

When you generate this clarity, you give yourself a sense of direction and purpose to hang on to right through all your dyings. This is, in essence, what many religions offer: a picture of realities beyond the physical and the application of this picturing or reality-generating process in daily life. You give yourself the idea that you have a place to go, that you will live on.

This idea can serve as a tool in increasing understanding of what is taking place when a challenge calling for a change is being faced and in mastering transition and death. Let's say this again and again:

YOUR CONSCIOUSNESS CAN LIVE ON.

In this sense,

YOU CAN WILL YOUR CONSCIOUSNESS TO LIVE ON. THIS IS YOUR RIGHT, YOUR CHOICE, YOUR PATH.

You, Your Essence

Yes—you can live on. The "you" you may think of as dying might die, but the "you" you are can still live on. It is important to distinguish between the two "you's":

WHAT THIS INVOLVES IS CLARIFYING FOR YOURSELF WHO YOU ARE: NOT WHAT YOU HAVE BEEN TOLD YOU ARE, NOT WHO YOU HAVE EXPERIENCED YOURSELF AS BEING IN THE MATERIAL PLANE, BUT WHO YOU—THE ESSENCE OF YOU—REALLY ARE.

Do not look to interactions with others to show you the whole of your own essence. Look within. Distill yourself from yourself, as if you were purifying a liquid for its purest essence. Know that:

- Your essence is not tied to a belief system; your essence is you.

- Your essence is not tied to a physical reality; your essence is you.
- Your essence is not tied to an emotional reality; your essence is you.

You Can Get There from Here

Your consciousness can find out about the limitations of limitations. Your consciousness can understand itself to be more than your physical body and thus more than any sensations the physical body feels, as well as more than your emotional body and thus more than any sensations the emotional body feels. The journey to the *true you* is neither long nor short. You are already there. Just know this and let yourself know this.

Always remember not to let anyone tell you that you cannot get there from here. This statement reveals the deep programming to believe in severe limitations. You can get anywhere you want from here, including to the true you. You just need to envision your journey and your destination. Envision clearly, and continuing clarifying your vision, with strong belief and precise intent. *Intent matters here!*

Envision Your Transition

Envision! Plan in order to generate your envisioning. Whether the death you face next is a within-life transition (such as a divorce, changing away from a way of life or breaking an addiction) or an actual physical death of the physical body, envision this transition. Take steps to plan the death of the body of behavior you have outgrown, the life you have outgrown.

Open your eyes to the forks and the windows of opportunity! These are everywhere. Identify the best openings or portals into your personally envisioned transformation. You will find this process easier than you might expect if you remain focused on your intent, your vision of your journey and destination.

Leaving the Body

Every moment of a lifetime offers us opportunities for understanding death, because we actually live and die and live every moment of every day. In some cultures, many of which are now disappearing from the face of the globe, there have been socially acceptable means of leaving the physical body. Not all of these methods involve the taking of drugs, the using of morphine pumps, the pulling of life-support-system plugs, or the administering of other forms of euthanasia (so-called "mercy killing"). Some indigenous peoples have had traditions allowing an individual who wishes to leave the body for good to formally decide to do so and then to lie down and die, taking one or a few twenty-four hour periods to accomplish this.

So-called "modern" humans may have forgotten that this noninvasive self-willed exit is an option. Perhaps this is related to our subtle fear of all transitions, whether in life or in physical death. Perhaps this is related to the efforts of far larger forces to keep us in the dark about this—perhaps this larger force is basically our own fear. Still, even "moderns" frequently, albeit subconsciously, practice this self-willed exit option, most often as a temporary leaving of the physical body during some of their dream states.

Leaving the body is actually quite simple. To do so, you must know the *keys*—the ways out—and you must know how to sever your own attachment, your own cords, to your own body. You must know you can survive. We have discussed the severance or detachment from the network of cords in previous volumes. Here we focus on the *actual getting out.*

Exercise 1.1: Floating Out

Lie or sit very still. Look at one of your hands. Imagine that you see your hand lifting out of itself, finger by finger, as if a ghost of your hand were leaving your hand.

As this ghost leaves, close your eyes. Use your imagination to follow your hand's ghost out of your body. Let your whole self follow. Float out bit by bit until you find yourself floating several feet above yourself. Linger there and look back at your body awhile.

Visualize two very fine silvery cords attaching you to your body, attaching to points of your choice on your body, such as one hooking to your forehead area, the other to your heart.

Form a triangle between yourself—your "ghost"—and these two points on your body. Hold this image awhile.

Then, following the path by which you exited, gently slip your consciousness back into your body.

Exercise 1.2: Getting Out

Stand up, if you can (otherwise, imagine that you are standing up). Focus on what we will call your vertical axis, which runs up and down your body in the direction of your physical spine.

Place your right hand (or imagine that you are placing your hand for these exercises) on the lowest part of your abdomen, just above the front of your genital area. Pull all your attention to the area of your body behind your hand. Hold this focus awhile.

Then place your left hand over your belly button, and pull all your focus there as you lift your right hand off the genital area. Hold your focus at this second point awhile.

Proceed to climb your vertical exit ladder in the same fashion, placing your hands as follows:

1. *Right hand over area just below the center of the rib cage. Hold your focus here awhile.*
2. *Left hand over area at center of chest, at the level of the heart. Hold your focus here awhile.*
3. *Right hand over throat. Hold your focus here awhile.*
4. *Left hand over forehead. Hold your focus here awhile.*
5. *Right hand a small distance from (over, not right on) the top of your head. Hold your focus here awhile.*
6. *Left hand extended way out over the top of the head. Hold your focus here awhile.*
7. *Now move your focus, your consciousness, far, far above the highest reach of the hand you have extended way over your head. Suck more of your consciousness into this point. Pull all of your consciousness to this high point on your vertical ladder. Hold. Hold. Hold yourself out there. . . . Hold, hold, hold.*
8. *Whoosh! You are out!*

Feel what this exit is like. Use your imagination, if this helps feel this exit. Understand how you have arrived out here. Think about what we are calling your vertical axis—your spine in your physical body. Hold the notion of your having a physical axis, what we can call a vertical axis, even when it is not vertical. Recognize that you can hold this notion whether or not your consciousness is connected to your physical body. Always know that you can follow your vertical axis out—out of a dimension—whether or not you have a body.

Now climb back into your body, back down the ladder you climbed to exit, step by step, hand by hand, slowly, with focus. First, bring your left hand to the point where you reached highest above your head. Second, bring your right hand a short distance over your head. Third, your forehead, then the throat area, then the heart area, the lower rib cage area, the belly, your lower abdomen area. Finally, focus on your feet to come all the way back in.

Exercise 1.3: Keying Out

You can unlock your self from your current reality, even from your physical existence, from your body. To do so, you can press the exit triggers, as these are a sort of combination lock. Here you will practice a form of this keying out with your hands. You will come to know you can do this with only your mental focus serving as your hands. Physical touch is actually not necessary to key out.

Use your two pointer fingers. Press firmly but not at all hard on each of the following points in the order listed below:

1. *Breathe in and hold. At same time, the left-hand finger presses in back, at the base of the back of the spine, and the right-hand finger presses in the lower front, opposite the left hand. Hold. Release. Then exhale.*
2. *Breathe in and hold. The arms are crossed, and the pointer finger of each hand presses the outer side of the center of the upper arm. Hold. Release. Then exhale.*
3. *Breathe in and hold. The left-hand finger presses in front at the base of the throat. The right-hand finger presses in back*

on the spinal cord opposite the left-hand finger. Hold. Release. Then exhale.

4. *Breathe in and hold. The pointer finger of each hand presses on its own side of the lower back of skull, above the top of the neck. Hold. Release. Then exhale.*
5. *Breathe in and hold. Both pointer fingers press in on the very center of the forehead. Hold. Release. Then exhale.*
6. *Breathe in and hold. Both pointer fingers press in on the very top center of the head. Hold. Release. Then exhale.*
7. *Breathe in and hold. Pointer fingers press on each other at the point as far as the fingers can reach above the top center of the head. As you pull those two fingers a few inches apart, gently but firmly feel a door click open. Like water flooding out of an abruptly opened dam, exhale and LEAP out beyond those fingers.*

Flow out of your body and anywhere you choose now. Feel this experience. Use your imagination to help feel this. Feel what it is like to be out. Get to know the accompanying sensations. There will be a time when you elect to move on and not return to your body. But for now, for this exercise, you will come back.

Place your right hand on top of your head and press hard. Come back in. Keep your right hand pressing there, and place your left hand over your lower abdomen. Press hard there too. Hold. Breathe deeply.

You may need to hold for quite a while. This depends upon the degree to which you convinced yourself of the fact that you were able to key out of your body during this exercise. You may want to have someone press with his or her palms on the bottoms of your feet to help you come all the way back in. If you have no one to do this, press or imagine you are pressing on the soles of your own feet.

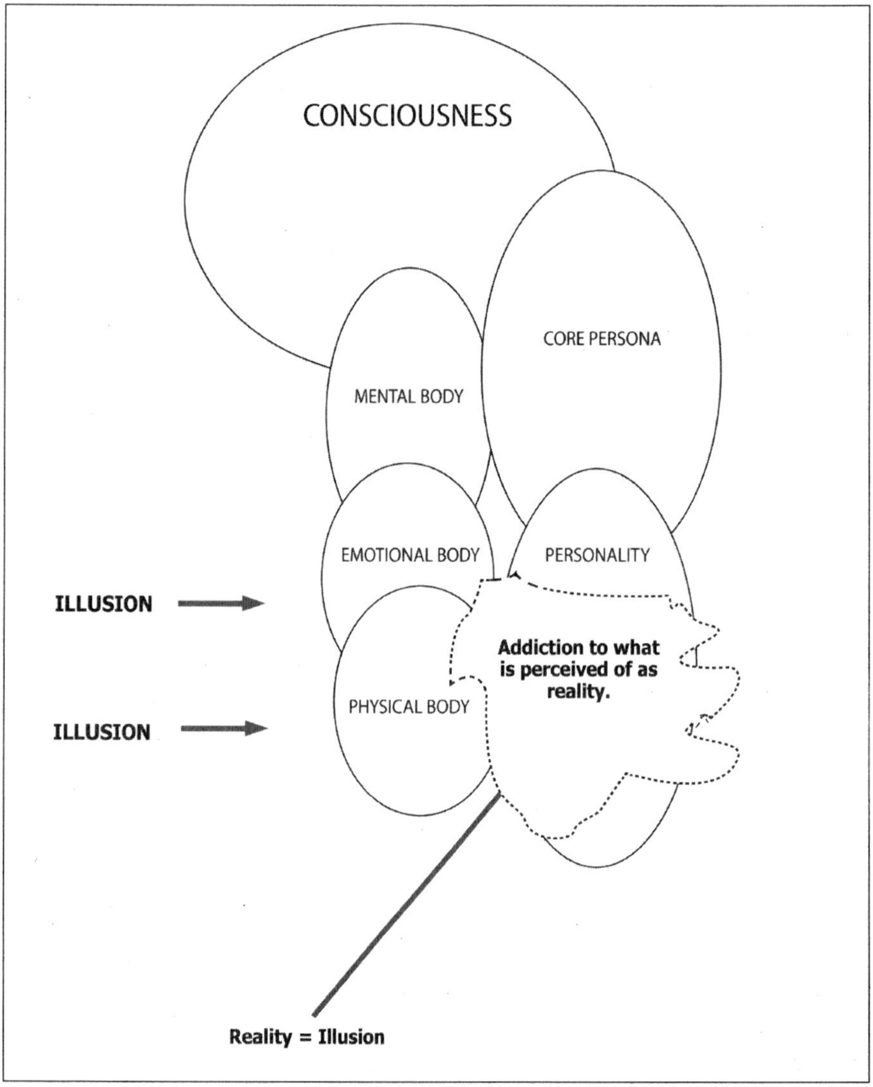

Figure 1.2. Consciousness, with the many bodies and realities it weaves.

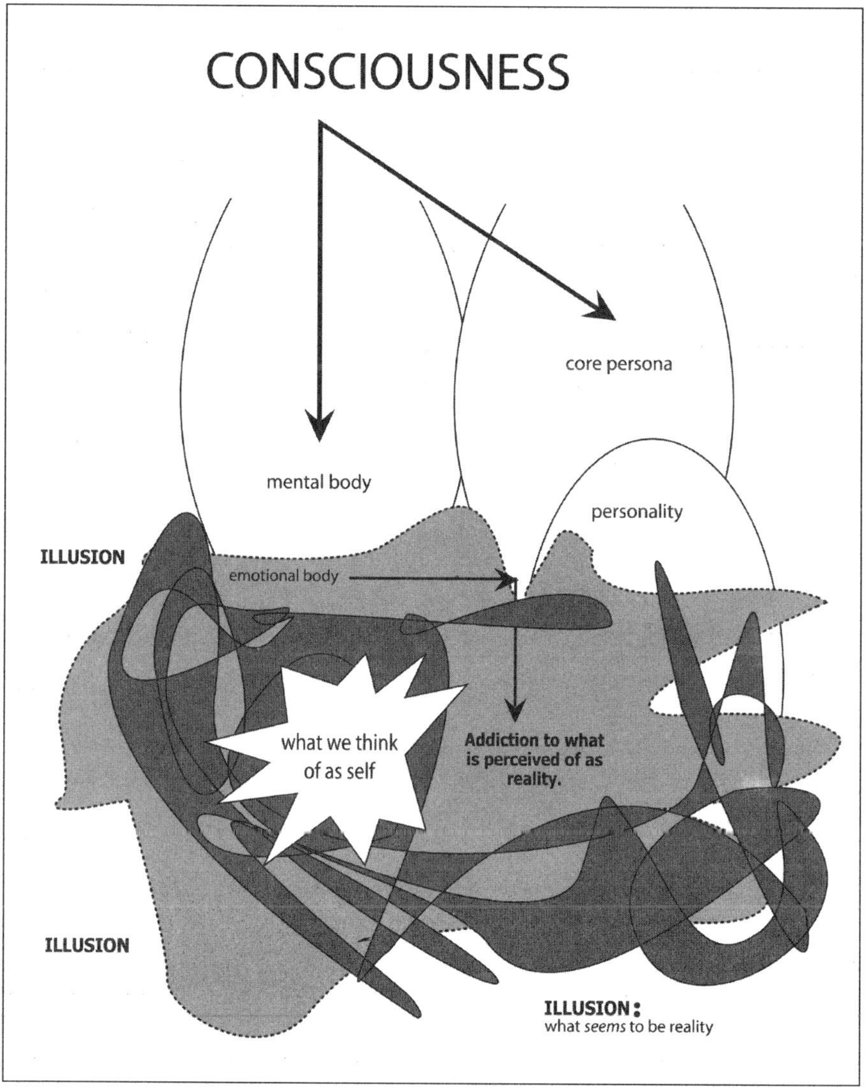

Figure 1.3. Consciousness and the entanglement it can be free of.

Chapter 2

Releasing the Old Matrix: Energetic Shedding

Distilled for purification are these juices of the Soma . . .

—"Hymn in Praise of Indra,"
the Rig-Veda

In a transition, the dissolution of the parts of the self that are not needed and are even a hindrance is an essential part of transitioning well—dying well—into a new cycle or phase of life, of reality. Think of the dissolution of unnecessary elements of the self as a shedding. It is like entering a house where shoes are not allowed. You take them off, shed them, to gain entry.

Shed to Facilitate a Dying

All minor and major deaths are a shedding. We have talked in previous volumes about the importance of being perceptive enough to spot windows of opportunity and, even before that, of being sensitive enough to know when you are at a fork in your road, at a choice point on your life (and death) path. Recall that there is usually a buildup to your coming to a fork or a window; there is usually a real need for shedding. It is easy to miss seeing this buildup for what it is, to miss seeing that you need to shed your shoes or your skin until you are either deep into the process of shedding, have completed the process or are well into a new life and looking back on the much-needed shedding that you stumbled into or perhaps must still fully complete.

The pressure to shed tends to sneak up on you. Whether it is the skin of an outgrown relationship, of an old behavior or of a troubled life, it takes awhile to notice and then to really admit that the skin has become far too tight—that you have outgrown it the way a snake outgrows its skin. It is a natural tendency, prior to understanding transition and death, to try to avoid many of your sheddings. However, you can get more out of the shedding process by recognizing when you are at its threshold and using wisely the energy that collects at the threshold of shedding.

Addiction to Reality Can Make Transition Difficult

The relatively obvious material-plane resistances to change are models of resistances to change that can occur in many dimensions of reality, even on less materially visible and materially invisible (to the material-physical eye) levels of reality. Selves, psyches and minds oft do not want to change—not very much. Even when minds think they want to change and convince themselves they have changed, they may cling to old thought patterns, old energy circuits, old forms of logic, old definitions of reality—old arrangements of energy, matrices, they have constructed.

That we can and do become addicted to our realities and that this addiction to reality can hinder—not necessarily serve to stop, but hinder—a smooth transition or death, is a simple but major understanding. We must be conscious of this tendency to cling to old patterns when nearing the end of a cycle, when the time has come to transition out of an old cycle, even when dying a physical death. We must understand that it is time to break the habit of, the addiction to the old reality and the addiction to the patterns that compose it.

This addiction to reality can have a profound physical component. This is due in large part to the literal wearing of actual grooves, deep neural pathways into the physical brain. Over time, as the same thought patterns (and the repeated behaviors these direct) are expressed again and again by the brain, deep neural pathways are worn into the paths from brain cell to brain cell and into the nervous system. These erode a sort of biological riverbed for themselves, a groove through which their movement is increasingly easy, increasingly habitual, increasingly automatic. This habit-feeding groove is one place where the nonphysical and the physical sides of the existence of a physical being may meet.

This is why it has been suggested that the surest way of removing old thought processes and conditionings is physical death. In physical death, the brain—with its physically burned-in programming—is shed, eliminated. While this is relatively true, the effective and complete shedding of burned-in patterning may have to be far more extensive. The biologically burned-in programming (burned in grooves or neural pathways) forms not only a biological pattern matrix but can also form a *parallel energetic matrix*—an organization of energy into patterns. This energetic matrix does not necessarily entirely expire at the time of physical death. Think of the energetic parallel to the biological patterning as the nonphysical twin of this pattern or matrix. Energy has arranged itself, been arranged over time, in a matrix that may hold when its physical counterpart dies—at least for a time.

We may even cling to this matrix while dying—mistakenly sensing, feeling, that our survival depends on the survival of this matrix. We might confuse ourselves with the matrices we have formed. This identity confusion is common and understandable. Uninformed physical, emotional and mental bodies may tend to cling to their old, deeply patterned matrices instead of releasing them, even when highly energetic shedding is necessary for ease of transition and for fully healing into a new reality. This shedding must reach far beyond the physical realm; it must reach into realms the physical self may have a hard time knowing exist while a physical self.

Clinging to a matrix in order to survive rather than die is not going to fuel survival. Instead, the opposite can take place. Hanging on to the matrix distracts you from what survives—from the core of the persona with its essence of self that is identified with pure consciousness.

YOU ARE NOT YOUR MATRIX.
YOU ARE YOU.
LET GO AND LIVE ON.

Options at Death

You can exercise various options during your "in life" transitions as well as during your physical death(s). You may want to choose options that enhance your power during transition. The power of any of your deaths is determined in these ways:

- in terms of the degree of energy the will of your consciousness identifies, collects and preserves through the dying process—this being directly related to the degree of letting go of all that may trap energy and weigh the consciousness down, of all the entangling cords to bodies and realities that must be left behind
- in terms of the degree to which your consciousness consciously identifies itself as distinct from all else once associated with the self, including the consciousness matrix
- in terms of the degree of sovereignty or free will your will collects and preserves during the dying process

Figure 2.1 diagrams the options you have at death along three basic death paths, ranging from the unintentional, powerless, entangled weak death, to the intentional, powerful, unencumbered strong death. Study this death path chart. (Note that suicide is not on this map of options. What is charted here in Figure 2.1 are *post*-death options.) Work at interpreting these options for yourself, making the options that you know you have what you wish them to be. Internalize this information. You may want to remind yourself of your interpretation of these options someday.

Note that you have many options at death. The level of awareness and energy you pump into your shedding process has great influence on the effects of this process. You can harvest a great amount of energy from your death. The more energetic your shedding, the greater your death release, the less encumbered your will, the more powerful your consciousness at the end of the process.

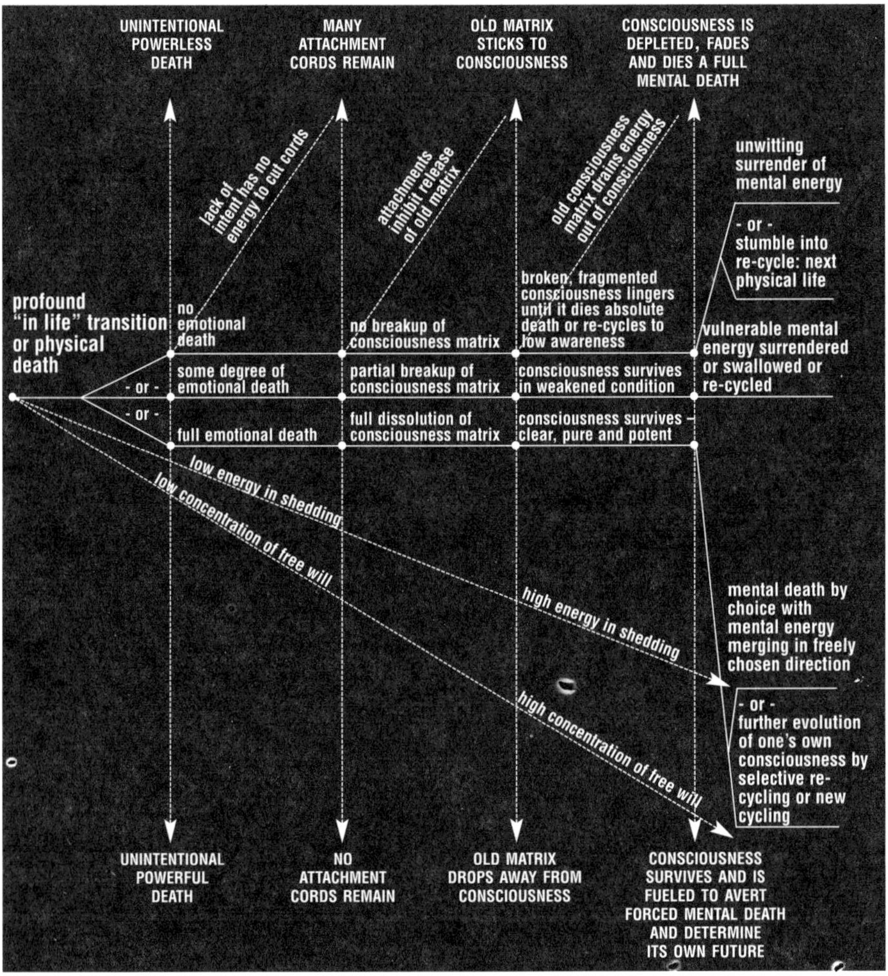

Figure 2.1. Options at death.

Exercise 2.1: Tracing Your Death Path

Study the death paths mapped in Figure 2.1. With a pencil and piece of paper, draw and label the death path you think you may want to follow. Use components of the paths diagrammed in Figure 2.1, invent your own components and even design your own path if you wish. Discuss (with yourself in your mind or aloud with another person) your reasons for designing your path as you have done. In your discussion, touch on the following topics:

- *emotional death*
- *the release of attachments and cords*
- *the old consciousness matrix*
- *the strength of the consciousness*
- *energy harvested in shedding*
- *increasing the concentration of one's free will*
- *distinguishing between giving over one's mental energy to another power or choosing to further retain one's mental energy to further evolve it*

Exercise 2.2: Undergoing Energetic Shedding

Close your eyes. Visualize a grid, or something like what you see when you look at graph paper. It will look something like this:

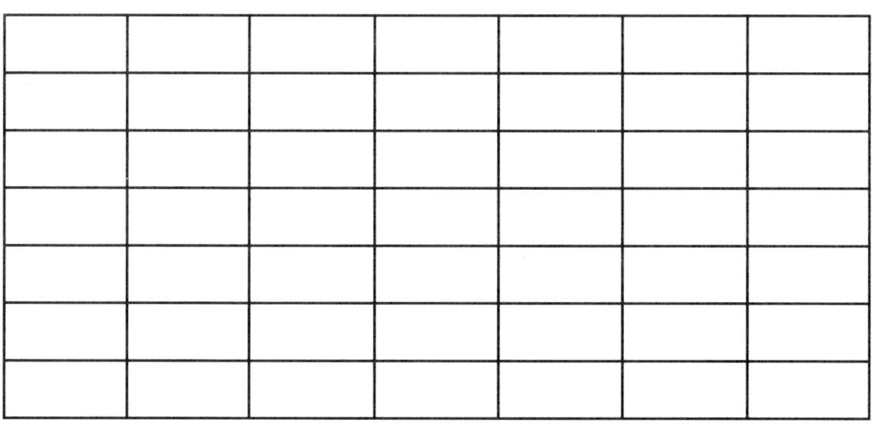

Now pour yourself into this grid, into the lines of this grid. Imagine that you are the lines of this grid. Build tension into the structure of this grid, as if this grid is trapping your energy. Tense your entire body as you identify with the tension in this grid. Hold the tension at its peak. Then light up the lines of the grid, release the grid, deconstruct, dissolve the lines. Transmute the now-freed energy (which was being held by the grid) to the highest form of energy or light it can become.

Try this again.

Repeat this exercise several times, each time increasing the level of tension at its peak. Feel the increase in the level of energy released when you dissolve your grid, which represents your matrix. You are escaping the matrix you created—you are being released.

Chapter 3

Dissolving the Self: At the Membrane

When upon thee Death fast approaches, fear not but know ye are master of Death. Relax thy body, resist not with tension. Place in the heart the flame of thy Soul. Swiftly then sweep it to the seat of the triangle.

—*Thoth,*
THE EMERALD TABLETS OF THOTH

After floating out of your old vessel for an indeterminate amount of time, you will begin examining this new "other-worldly" terrain. There you will find all kinds of energy bundles as well as openings and windows in the space around you. You may continue to float in that same space or you might find that you move toward and even through one of these windows.

Embrace Shifts and Transitions

This is the case for shifts and transitions while living in your present life, as well as for physical-death transitions. The parallels are everywhere around you:

JUST LOOK

This is more than just "reaching" into another dimension of your reality. Many people may do this sort of "reaching" as imaginary, dream state or casual mental exploration. However, fully moving through a window into another dimension of your life is a *full shift of your location* to that dimension, rather than an exploratory reaching from one dimension into another. (Of course, the exercises in this volume encourage exploratory reaching for the purposes of exercising the consciousness.)

When we say "full" shift, we mean full shift in what the consciousness defines as being its reality. In other words, your consciousness—you—is whatever and wherever it chooses itself to be. Your consciousness remains static, in the same state, or it goes into transition in the manner it chooses. While your physical and emotional bodies experience their biological, social and emotional environments, your consciousness may monitor the experience but is not affected by it unless it consciously chooses to be.

Moving the entire consciousness through a window into another dimension (of its reality or even of itself, as these are in essence the same) entails something like the crossing of a membrane. Think of this membrane as the skin of the next reality or dimension. This skin is something like a cell wall in that it is semipermeable, only allowing some of what seeks to pass into or to penetrate it.

Go to Pure You

Now let's look more closely at this membrane crossing or

transition: Although each window, or transition, has its specific characteristics, the basic requirement for complete passage is a selective dissolution of the old *matrix of self*, the old arrangement or consciousness matrix, the one you formatted during your most recent lifetime in another dimension of reality. Indeed, there is this option of *selective dissolution*—dissolving the matrix but not the consciousness—as the essence of the self can be and frequently is maintained. This essence of self is what is left there at the core when all the fluff is cleared away. This is where your core persona is revealed—the core persona of your consciousness itself:

PURE YOU!

Recognize Preliminary and Eventual Dissolutions

Each of the stages of death is a step in this selective transitional dissolution of old self. By "old self," what is meant is the trappings of the old self that have been formed during third-dimensional, material-plane existence. By "selective transitional dissolution," what is meant is the shedding of unnecessary and undesirable iterations accumulated during material-plane existence—a shedding to best facilitate transition. This sheds the stuff that has attached itself to the persona; this sheds the surface personality.

As explained elsewhere in this volume, full physical death is a wonderful model of the stages of dissolution necessary to go through any major change in one's self. Recall that the first death in physical death is the basic death, that of the physical body. This death can be quick, or long and drawn out. When this death is complete, there still remain the emotional and mental bodies.

Eventually, the physically dead individual must die the second death, the emotional death, leaving behind all emotional connection, all cording to both the physical and emotional planes, and move on. As covered in Volumes One and Two, this letting go is a critical and challenging process for many a soul. It takes clarity and force of will to die a graceful and powerful emotional death. The soul senses that what comes after emotional death is the option of mental death, the option of dissolving or dissipating any unnecessary surface mental energy—excess mental energy that lingers even *after* the emotional energy has been shed, mental energy assumed and structured during the recent and previous incarnations and formations.

See Mental Death as Purification of the Consciousness

As it is frequently misunderstood, mental death warrants close examination. Mental death is not a death; mental death is not the death of the consciousness. Rather, it is the *further purification* of it. Mental death is said by some to be the third death. It has been said that very few spirits are "evolved enough" to succeed in fully completing this third death and, in so doing, cross the threshold beyond the death cycle. It is also said that most fail at this death and therefore must re-cycle involuntarily and without selectivity again and again until someday they will finally succeed. *Yet this is not necessarily the case!*

Let's rethink mental death, reframe it as *purification of the consciousness*. As Figure 2.1 indicates, there is another way of explaining what happens at this third stage of death. There are actually degrees of mental transition or death, each involving a different amount of shedding of the consciousness matrix. Lesser degrees shed less; greater degrees shed almost all or all of the consciousness matrix. *Note that this is not a shedding of the consciousness.*

The lesser degrees of mental death are entangled with incomplete emotional death. Most who are naive (non-expert) about dying manage only a small degree of mental purification, if any. Say that the naive dying person hangs on to the emotional body, resisting the release of some of the old cords or ties. Effective mental purification is next to impossible when the emotional body has not been shed. This is because emotionality (and the intermingled personality) must be shed before surface mentality can be released.

Those who are still even a little emotionally corded enter the third phase of death corded, tied, even handcuffed to the old life. This is a futile condition, especially in cases where the physical body is already dead or is so uninhabitable that it can never be returned to in a functional way. Clinging to (or having someone else force the "clinging to") an unlivable damaged vessel drags the power of one's consciousness down. This may cause the mental purification transition to be sloppy and vulnerable to outside interference. Only a small degree of the consciousness matrix can be shed while this matrix is still emotionally entangled—maybe 2 or 3 percent of the total possible shedding can occur.

Should you choose to, you will recall the essence of these words when you are into your second death, your emotional death. Staying conscious during this process will allow you to remain the captain of your journey. Keep in mind that we are not talking about staying biologically (or medically) conscious here. Whether or not biologically or medically conscious, the consciousness itself can stay alert. It is up to that consciousness to do so, to maintain itself through any transition. You will benefit by staying conscious, because an emotionally trapped, entangled but disembodied (physically dead) being may have a weakened consciousness while in this trapped state. (If you hear those around you saying you are not conscious, just remember that they are speaking about your biologically based consciousness, your biological body and brain, not your core consciousness.)

Aim to carry your conscious state into the next phase of your transition, beyond the emotional death to the lower-mental-body shedding or death. The effective shedding of the old unnecessary parts of your mental body's matrix may be inhibited. (Moreover, in your weakened state, forces that seek to use your energy for their own evolutionary purposes—which may not be the purposes of the evolution of your consciousness or of that of humanity—can easily take over.) Break free of the physicalities, emotionalities and surface mentalities that bind you. Release the webs and matrices to clarify the pure consciousness, *your* pure consciousness. The part of you that you choose to shed can die—and *you* can survive.

Understand Degrees of Mental Death

You want the shedding of your surface mentality to be completed when, where and in the manner and to the degree that *you* choose. It is, after all, your own mental-body transition. You do not necessarily want a complete mental death just because you have the option. Moreover, the timing of your mental death should be *your* decision. The way to make such a decision, when you are suspended in an unattached and disoriented state, is to be quite conscious. (Again, this is not necessarily biologically conscious.)

Figure 2.1 indicates the path toward higher consciousness—evolving, freewill-promoting death. (Refer to the lower right-hand corner of Figure 2.1, where it states that "consciousness survives and is fueled to avert forced mental death and determine its own future.") Let's say you elect this path. Once well into this freewill path and up to the point of freely determining whether to turn your energy over to a higher power or to continue to evolve it for yourself, you have yet another process to conduct: *You must dissolve at the membrane of the next reality, the next dimension.* This dissolving is further clarification of the consciousness.

Dissolve at the Membrane

As mentioned earlier, each dimension of reality has a surface or skin that does not allow everything that approaches it through. (Again, it matters not whether this "skin" is a construct of your own consciousness or something external to it, as these are in essence one and the same at this core level.) For you to pass successfully and purely on into a higher, less dense, more pure dimension, you must be unattached to what you are leaving behind. All cords must have been released; the entire emotional body must have been shed.

Do not think you can slip safely through the membrane with the unnecessary parts of your old consciousness matrix. Information and energy will not be arranged the same way in the next dimension; therefore, there is no reason for anything but your core pure consciousness itself to go there. Cross (get through) the membrane, then reformat if your consciousness elects to.

Even an entirely released consciousness must work to dissolve at the membrane. Imagine a salt crystal moving from air to water. It must dissolve to suspend itself in the water; otherwise, it floats and crusts around the edges of the water. *The extraneous, added-on parts of your matrix must dissolve at the membrane of your new reality for you to fully enter the next dimension or kingdom of reality.* Knowing your essence, your pure consciousness, in advance is helpful.

Exercise 3.1: Clarifying Your Essence

Spend quite awhile attempting to find, to know the essence of you. What are you without your surface identity, your surface personality, your surface feelings, your friends and family, your history, your commitments? Sense the core, the basic character of your energy. Get to know this inner and true nature of your self. Strip down to your pure, unencumbered essence and what consciousness of the essence is carried there. When you feel you have even begun to clarify your essence—to find you *minus your physical and emotional bodies,* you *minus your personality—then hold there.*

Exercise 3.2: Dissolving at the Membrane

Now be in the center of this core essence of you. Direct your essence to spread out, becoming even less dense than it already is. Dissolve to minuscule nonphysical bits, equal bits of yourself. Know that each bit is all of you. You are not broken in pieces here; each bit is the whole you. Contemplate this state of being for a while . . . you, in pieces, each a piece of a whole you.

Now have all your bits approach a wall of clear skin. The skin appears to you to be the wall of a giant bubble. You must get into the bubble through its skin, through its pores.

Be just one of your tiny bits representing your entire purified consciousness. Move toward this skin, this membrane. See the opening, the pore in this membrane that you will take this bit of your essence through. Approach the pore in the membrane.

Get right up in front of this pore. See that this pore has a membrane across it too. This membrane is thinner than the skin around the pores. This special membrane is a sieve-like barrier, only allowing through all bits of essence that are unformatted, that carry no grid or matrix from the previous dimension.

See yourself as stripped down of all extraneous projections, grids, attachments and ideas about your self or reality. Clarify and purify your essence, as if you are a drop of water unmuddying itself, a light changing from murky to crystal clear.

Feel crystalline and sharp in your essence. Sharpen. Sharpen your essence. Sharpen and refine. Hold awhile as if perched on a high mountain or on the outside windowsill of a very tall building. Sharpen your essence and perch. Hold this perch. Take a soft breath in and hold it in as you perch, balancing your crystal-clear purified essence before the special membrane. Hold your breath a little longer. Then, suddenly, feel as if you are melting. Relax and release your breath. Melt until you are almost nothing.

Slip, like a tiny, crystal clear, microscopic river, right through the membrane of the pore of the skin of the next dimension. As the river of you crosses through the membrane, feel as though you are being combed through and through.

Know that your arrival on the other side has occurred when the combing sensation ceases.

Congratulations! You have made it through to the other side.

See Membranes

Sieve-like membranes across openings, pores or windows to other dimensions of reality (and thus to other dimensions of your consciousness) are all around you. Once you train your eyes to see them and your self to sense them, you will be amazed at how many there are. You may wonder why more individuals living in physical bodies do not just slip or fall through into another dimension by mistake and never return. Few physically embodied beings slip through, because few are sufficiently reduced down to a pure-enough essence to simply seep through the sieve. And few understand how to melt, although this is actually extremely simple with practice.

When you or someone you are close to is about to cross over to the other side to another dimension, you may notice out of the corner of your eye a membrane come into focus in your vicinity. Sometimes images, likenesses (designed in a way your consciousness can recognize) of long-gone friends and family appear faint and semi-material just on the other side of the membrane, as if they are waiting to coach you (or whoever is in transition) through to the beyond. Notice how sublimely detached they appear. This is not surprising. Your arrival into the next dimension is greeted with far more detached anticipation than your heavily corded departure from this one.

Chapter 4

Retaining the Consciousness

. . . the place between thine eyebrows, the place where the memory of life must hold sway. Hold thou thy flame here in thy brain-seat until the fingers of Death grasp thy Soul.

—*Thoth,*
THE EMERALD TABLETS OF THOTH

A highly trained being, practiced in the transition and death technologies explained in this *Continuity of Life* series, can leave the physical vehicle quite consciously. In full awareness, that individual can fully preserve the continuity of consciousness while moving through any transition, including from the physical plane to the "after physical death" states. You can do this relatively well, whether or not you have received intensive training, especially if you can stay conscious and remember that your emotions and feelings are not the core of your consciousness but rather part of an emotional body that you are shedding. You will be helped by the knowledge that you, your consciousness—*what you really are*—does not die.

Remember that the thread of awareness is a finely woven fiber, formed of very fine filaments of a very pure light. This precious and vulnerable thread is all you have of yourself once you have unraveled your consciousness matrix, reduced it and separated it into minuscule bits, to cross through the membrane of the opening to the other side—to the new reality. In your unbundled state of many minuscule bits, you are the ball of yarn unwound. You are the weaving pulled off the loom, the grid, warp and the weft indistinguishable. You are your consciousness in its most naked state—unraveled filaments of energy, raw light.

Appreciate Consciousness

Once you have made it this far, you can know that you have conducted a conscious dying—so far. Yet there is still more to this great adventure. Think a moment about the importance of conscious dying. As valuable as conscious dying may be, it takes concentration to understand exactly what it is that is of value. Why is this understanding so difficult to come by? Because consciousness itself is elusive. It cannot be contained; it has no boundaries.

Consciousness cannot be bottled and sold; it is not in itself a compound or a psychoactive drug. Although many things affect the consciousness matrix and many individuals claim to be able to measure the effects of these things on consciousness, consciousness itself cannot be measured. Consciousness is not measurable in terms of something like "brain size" or a number such as "IQ" (intelligence quotient). Third-dimensional characterizations of consciousness do not characterize consciousness because consciousness is not a third-dimensional, material-plane thing, even though it registers some of its effects there.

Your consciousness is your reach beyond the particular dimensions in which your physical and emotional bodies and your surface mentalities live. Your consciousness is larger than what you may know it to be or sense it as being.

YOU ARE FAR MORE THAN YOU MAY HAVE BEEN TOLD YOU ARE. YOU ARE YOUR EXPANSIVE CONSCIOUSNESS.

It is mistakenly assumed that persons who are medically diagnosed and labeled "severely retarded," "senile," "brain-dead" or "comatose" are not very or not at all conscious. This is an understandable material-plane error in perception. The consciousness of beings who appear to be "semi-" or "un"conscious is not being expressed to any great degree—or to any degree at all—through the physical vehicle, the physical body. This does not mean that the consciousness is dead. It may be overly connected to its consciousness matrix and unable to move on.

The consciousness of that individual might linger nearby or be far away. The consciousness matrix once maintained by that being's consciousness may be entirely intact, intact to some degree or completely dissolved. Typical material plane tests will not reveal the degree to which that consciousness matrix is still bundled. Again, this is because consciousness is not a material thing and the consciousness matrix is not a material thing.

Know, with full resolve to really know, that your consciousness is neither material nor emotional. Think in terms of retaining your consciousness through the shedding of the physical, the emotional and even the mental cord networks; through the dissolution of the consciousness matrix; and through the crossing over of or moving through the membrane. Remember that your life experience (administered by the matrix, arrangement or formatting of your consciousness) is your unreduced, impure surface mentality and *not* your pure consciousness.

IF YOU TRY TO TAKE ANYTHING WITH YOU THAT IS NOT PURE YOU, THAT IS NOT YOUR PURE CORE CONSCIOUSNESS, YOU WILL BE HELD BACK, DRAGGED DOWN, FRAGMENTED, WEAKENED, CONFUSED AND LOST.
YOU CANNOT GET THERE FROM HERE IF YOU GO AS ANYTHING BUT WHO YOU REALLY ARE.
SO REVEAL YOURSELF TO YOURSELF.
SEE YOUR ESSENCE TO SURVIVE.

Exercise 4.1: Retaining Your Consciousness

Find yourself passing through the membranes of the pores of the skin of the next dimension. Remember, you have become many bits of your essence to do this. As you pass through the pores in the membrane, feel your entire consciousness housed in, stored in each reduced and purified bit of yourself. Contemplate this replication of yourself for a moment. There you are again and again and again!

Now move through the membrane of the pore. You have no body and thus no physical eyes here, so use your inner eye, the one you trained while still in a body, to see every bit of this process. See each bit of yourself being combed by the fine sieve of the membrane. Feel every minor sensation involved in this combing process. Continue into the next exercise.

Exercise 4.2: Clustering Your Conscious Bits

See each bit of yourself arrive on the other side. Recognize each bit of your self and gravitate all these bits toward each other. Have your bits begin to cluster. Have your bits greet each other consciously. Yes! Consciously! You are still conscious!

Chapter 5

Rebundling: Dance of (Re)Creation

It is a strange awakening to find sky inside you and beneath you and above you so that your spirit is one with the sky. . . .

—*Thomas Merton,*

ENTERING THE SILENCE

Be immensely patient with your self. This death technology is a lot to take in. It is so profoundly simple yet intensely demanding; it is so vague and yet so clear. And you are learning to navigate the boundless infinity, the infinite potential of your consciousness.

Ask the Question and Dance Your Creation

Your mastery of death will unfold within you as your interdimensional consciousness grows in its awareness of itself. Your instinctive longing for the incredible journey into the glistening beyond, into *your* beyond, will eventually bring on the complete shedding of all your previous attachments and the full dissolution of your old consciousness matrix. And indeed you will eventually manage to dissolve into whole bits of yourself and transport your essence, your purified consciousness, across the membrane.

But will you ever pull yourself back together again? This is the most significant decision you will make on your journey. Will you reassemble, rebundle these minuscule bits of your self? Will you spin a recollected consciousness out of what you have taken through the membrane?

By asking this question at the point in your journey when you have just managed to cross the membrane, you have accomplished something tremendous: You are on the "other side," and you are still conscious or you would not be able to ask yourself such a question!

Now is your opportunity to choose *of your own free will* whether to:

- disperse the bits of your pure core consciousness into the particular dimension and location within that dimension that you have come to, thereby dissolving your pure core self, or,
- rebundle the bits of your pure core consciousness and remain your self and journey on through the cosmos as your pure core self.

Rebundle Your Consciousness

Once you have clustered the bits of your self on the new (new-to-you) side of the membrane, in order to actually rebundle, you must have your bits engage in the following steps:

- Arrive at a common intent to rebundle.
- Pull the cluster of bits of your self in tighter together.
- Begin spinning each bit in what seems to be a clockwise direction at its base and a counterclockwise direction at its top.
- Increase the spinning of these bits until a high humming is heard by each bit and among the bits.
- Have the spinning bits form an oceanlike wave together by moving, oscillating en masse, up, up, up, and then rolling, rolling, rolling outward, and then coasting down, down, down.
- Continue making such waves repeatedly, involving all your bits, as they are of common mind.
- Increase the power and motion and speed of these waves.
- As each wave rolls, begin to form a spiral at its center.
- Have these spirals become increasingly powerful with a stronger and stronger suction force being formed within each successive wave.
- Have this suction begin to overpower the wave, pulling more and more of the bits of the wave (the bits of you) into its center.
- Have this suction eventually have all the bits pressing in on themselves so tightly that they compress and merge!
- Become one rebundled consciousness, a large ball of light.

Exercise 5.1: Dancing the Wave

Visualize your self a cluster of bits of your pure consciousness. Now proceed through the steps listed above. You may want to have someone read these to you.

Exercise 5.2: Arriving Again

When you have completed the last step, tell yourself: "I am consciousness rebundled, re-created." Feel the meaning, the essence of this statement. Feel your essence. Congratulations—you have just completed your personal dance of creation!

Chapter 6

Reformatting the Self: Free of Cords

Even if science—physical science or occult science—were to discover the necessary condition or means for an indefinite survival of the body, still, if the body could not adapt itself so as to become a fit instrument of expression for the inner growth, the soul would find some way to abandon it and pass on to a new incarnation. The material or physical causes of death are not its sole or its true cause; its true inmost reason is the spiritual necessity for the evolution of a new being.

—*Sri Aurobindo,*
THE LIFE DIVINE

You wake up dead—or do you? Once you would have thought so, but now you know better. There you are, having traversed the limits of the material plane, having transformed to a most unbundled, evaporated, released state, devoid of all that you most considered your self to be prior to this point, and then into a rebundled but still quite naked consciousness. Now the challenge is to *reformat* this rebundling of your self. Now you will discover what it means to (re)format a consciousness matrix.

Reformatting Your Self

We call this reformatting, because time and again on your great journey you will be called upon to dissolve and then rebundle and then, after that, reformat. Reformatting is beyond all you have done so far. We have discussed what is involved in releasing the old matrix, the old bundle of energy networks, the programming loops, patterns and connections to the web of interpersonal, physical, emotional and intellectual worlds. We have discussed what is involved in crossing over and then rebundling.

Once all this is completed, you have a further choice. You can either remain bundled but unformatted and have your consciousness naked, or you can *fashion a new consciousness matrix*—reformat. You can build this insulating energetic structure around what has been rebundled, out of the photonlike particles of your essence that have made it through the membrane because they successfully detached. You can call back to center, back into focus, and organize the particles of your self that have detached from your matrix (that have detached from your web of cords, as well as from the web's ties to the physical, emotional and intellectual particles you have now left behind).

The particles of your self, your pure essence, that you will find "on the other side" will be those that have successfully made the full LEAP into another dimension. These particles of your self are the ones that are fully purified, fully detached, and thereby are able to increase their frequency of motion to LEAP into a higher dimension. These particles have entirely de-physicalized, dematerialized.

Now, in this new dimension, in this nonphysical and non-emotional state, these particles can reorganize themselves. These particles may elect to form a new consciousness matrix. This matrix can shield them. Pull together and organize even these well-filtered particles very carefully, so that you take with you into your new life only the particles of your self you consciously choose and only the ones that will fit your new format.

Consciously Reformat

This information regarding the reformatting of the self can be applied in all stages of life and in any of life's and death's transitions. Once you begin to appreciate in a whole new way the concepts that your major transitions are all deaths and that you can reformat yourself any way you want to after your transition and death processes, you will gain power over the course of your life, your deaths and your evolution. As you grow in this understanding, you gain an increasing say in the use of your energy. Remember that you are continuously cultivating—manufacturing, generating, formatting, harvesting and transforming—your energy. So long as you take responsibility for your energy, you can have a positive say in its arrangement and use.

Understand your right to access and arrange energy. You can access the energy flowing through you and through any dimension of reality at any moment you choose. This is free energy. You are part of it. You help manufacture it. You help format it. You release it, contribute it, into reality. You have as much right to energy as anyone or anything else. You have as much right to determine its format in your domain of consciousness.

Apply Only Right Use of Free Will

Yet with your rights come your responsibilities. Energy is always arranging and rearranging. Your own energy is always rearranging. In this sense, there are always at least minor transitions with all their sheddings and dyings under way. To abandon even the most minor of these dyings, to be at any time unconscious, is a surrender of responsibility.

Always remember that each shift across a dimensional barrier or membrane—even location within a physical reality in which you are presently living—is a LEAP. You must always be alert to the *sensations that accompany any large or small transition and its formation-shifting.* Do not let these sensations sneak up on you and take you over. The right use of your free will is exercised by your alert consciousness.

Recognize Formation Shifting

Once your dimension-shifting is under way, you may sense that you are indeed traversing dimensions. You might feel sensations similar to growing older, growing younger, dying and/or being born. Or you may feel as if you are transforming, expanding, evaporating or bursting in all directions. It is quite common to feel compression as you dimension-shift. Know that the sense of intense flatness, the compression you may feel, is merely a passing state (unless you choose to stay in that compressed form).

If you find yourself in the midst of what feels to be an intensely compressed experience, let time pass. After a while, you may see some light beaming out of the density or darkness of this compression. This "light" might appear in the form of splashes of water or pieces of broken glass. Imagine that you become one of those bits of water or pieces of broken glass. *Let yourself splash and shatter.*

When you have allowed whatever remains of your old matrix to dissolve or even shatter, you can consider putting yourself back together. Be determined not to reinstate old cords, old programs, old loops. Many of the old programs cannot be entirely reinstated without the cords they formed in the material world. But do be careful not to unconsciously reinstate all or pieces of old patterns—old patterns of victimhood, of subservience, of fear, of aggression, of domination, of addiction, or other patterns that may linger, patterns that have not been entirely dissolved. Some will call these karmic patterns. Some will say that this is the moment that karma can be rewritten or one of the prime moments in which the opportunity to rewrite karma is most available.

An aware core self—a core consciousness aware of its dimensional locale and aware of the extent to which its particles have actually disbursed its particular crystallized matrix patternings—can be determined and careful to avoid reinstating bits of old bodies, patterns and matrices. Pay attention. You will see what of you has been disbursed, how much of it you wish to recollect and how it can be recollected. When reformatting the self, take care. Pick and choose and arrange consciously. You are what you create yourself to be. You move on in the form you choose to.

Exercise 6.1: Reformatting Practice

Close your eyes. Imagine that you are dissolving. As you dissolve, find that what there is of you now is evaporating. As you evaporate, find that what there is of you now is dispersing, spreading out.

Disperse as far as you can imagine dispersing. Feel your consciousness dispersing.

Continue dispersing until you are told to reformat. When you are told to reformat, see and feel yourself snap back into your physical body.

Reformat.

Exercise 6.2: Repeating Reformats

Do the above exercise several times in a row, each time dispersing your consciousness further and each time reformatting with more force. Note the expand-contract callisthenic being practiced here.

With each successive reformatting, try to leave out additional bits of your lower self that may carry (at least traces of) old patterns.

Chapter 7

LEAPing to the Next Dimension: LEAP Level Four

Once upon a time, I . . . dreamt I was a butterfly. . . . Suddenly, I awoke. . . . Now I do not know whether I was then a man dreaming I was a butterfly, or whether I am now a butterfly dreaming I am a man.

—Chuang Tzu (Zhuang-Zi),
THE CHUANG TZU

Humans are preoccupied with their bodies. They feed their bodies. They dress and decorate their bodies. They exercise their bodies, not always understanding that the exercise to which they subject their bodies is really a model for the exercise to which they desire to subject their consciousnesses. Yes, the symmetry attained by certain physical exercise is the balance they seek; the muscle strength they attain lifting weights is the strength they seek; the endurance and stamina they attain in aerobic exercise is the endurance and stamina they seek; the flexibility and agility they attain in stretching their bodies, moving to music and participating in sports that require quick agile movements is the flexibility, agility and alertness they seek—all for their nonphysical selves, their consciousnesses.

Train the Consciousness

What you do with your body can indeed be training for your nonphysical self, your consciousness. Your physical calisthenics mirror those *consciousness calisthenics* you seek. You are preparing for multidimensional journeying and for the LEAPs you will take as you go through minor and major transitional and dimensional shifts, sheddings and dyings.

A LEAP (light-energy-action process) is a movement from one dimension to the next. A LEAP is usually best and most efficiently brought about when consciously constructed. Each LEAP is, of course, a death, as each shift in "daily life" and in "end of life" dimension or reality is a death. The more trained the dying being is, the cleaner and more potent the death LEAP. You can master the LEAP and use it any time you wish, in any living or any physical death.

Exercise 7.1: Knowing Dimensional Expansion

Close your eyes. Be a point, a single point in space. Feel that you have no height, width or depth.

Now stretch this point that you are out into a long, thin line. Feel that you have only one dimension: length. Float this way awhile.

Stretch the line out, spread it out, into a row of lines or a plane, a big flat plane. Float this way awhile.

Now pile many planes onto your plane, making them stack themselves, sandwich themselves into a cube. Feel that you now have length, width and depth. Float this way awhile, as a three-dimensional object . . .

Move this three-dimensional object that you are, this cube, through time, with its length, width and depth each moving through time in its own different direction. Do this and see that you undergo an incredible expansion! You feel large and limitless, free of the confines of the boundaries of the three-dimensional form of the cube you were trapped in. This is the time-burst typical of the full fourth-dimensional energy expansion. This time-burst signifies the LEAP into the fourth dimension.

Hold for the next exercise.

Exercise 7.2: Raising to the Next Level

Exercise your consciousness a bit more. Now take that energy expansion, that time-burst, that LEAP, and raise it yet another level. Expand in some new way, a way you cannot exactly describe in words.

Do not think about this too hard. Just let your mind review the nature of the mental shift, the LEAP across dimensions, that is needed to go from the idea of a point to the idea of a line or a straight piece of thread; from the idea of a line to the idea of a plane or a flat piece of paper; from the idea of a plane to a cube; from the idea of a cube to the time-burst; from the idea of the time-burst to something that is yet another and still more expansive burst beyond that.

Leap to the Next Dimension

The LEAP into another dimension is at once incredibly complex and amazingly simple. It is complex because it involves the harnessing of many physical and metaphysical energies. It is simple because you have within you, buried deep within you, all the knowledge required to make such a LEAP.

All that is required is the triggering of your memory. This is what we seek to do here. Remember.

You are already completely competent in the complete movement of your full consciousness from one dimension of reality to another. You already have the skills to LEAP out of your present dimension of reality—your present phase of life or your present physical body—to another reality. Learn what you know:

GO CONSCIOUS.

PART II

HOW TO NAVIGATE THE CHANGING, HEALING, SHIFTING AND ASCENSION OUT OF AN EXISTING PHYSICAL CONDITION OR REALITY

Part II of this volume journeys further into what it means to navigate change, transition and healing. Here, physical death is framed as a metaphor for shifting realities, for healings of realities and for what it is—death of the physical body. Within the realm of this metaphor, the symbolic and actual passage into and then through the nonphysical is described, diagrammed and symbolically experienced, training the consciousness for the conscious journeys into different physical, emotional and mental conditions it can make.

Chapter 8

Re-cycling and Redescending: Pros and Cons

Think of all the bones that have accumulated on the face of the earth. . . . All those billions of men and women who have discarded their bones, their skin, their fat.

—*Omraam Mikhaël Aïvanhov,*
FRUITS OF THE TREE OF LIFE:
THE CABBALISTIC TRADITION

Clearly, conscious transition out of the physical body is a metaphor for all transitions we make consciously (including any transition from one physical condition to another, such as those taking place in healing). Purposefully shifting to a new reality requires the purposeful navigation of transition. Knowledge about navigating transition, knowing the keys to effectively navigate transition, promotes conscious transition at all points in life and death. Let's continue to look at the transition out of the physical body (which accompanies physical death) as both metaphor and actuality.

Transition as Both Metaphor and Actuality

Let's say that once out of your body, you can elect to have the opportunity to decide of your own free will to move on and ascend independently to new realities, new domains for your consciousness, or to merge with another consciousness. Or as Figure 8.1 suggests, you can also choose to *redescend*—to drop back or *re-cycle* into the dimension you have just left, to return to a previous condition or something akin to it.

This conceptual understanding of *conscious change* is relevant to healing, as well as to other important "in life" and "in death" transitions. Healing of the ailing physical body can be conducted on the biological, physical level, and it can be conducted on the nonphysical level. One means of nonphysical healing is *conscious pattern extension*.

Modern medicine will eventually embrace the power of healing patterns from outside physicality. Human consciousness is moving toward realizing its potential to heal a physical condition by exiting that condition (or body), then working on the nonphysical components of the patterns and matrices that extend past that body to correct any troubled energies, then allowing this correction to be reflected back in physicality by redescending. Healing takes on new dimensions when it requires no medicine, no surgery, no physical intervention.

When you redescend—or better stated, when your consciousness moves back to a setting it previously left—you are *cycling back* into the type of cycle you have just completed. When there has been little or no healing of troubled energy patterns, redescending is virtually repetition. In this vein, one might say that if you are leaving a physical lifetime, you might tend to seek a replay of the cycles your energy had followed

Figure 8.1. To ascend or re-cycle.

during that lifetime. If you are leaving a troubled relationship, you may tend to fall back into old patterns of relations with the same or a new person. If you are leaving an addiction to a drug, you may tend to fall back into a parallel addiction, sometimes without seeing this tendency coming. Leaving a state of "dis-ease" (any state away from "ease") and then redescending back into it may involve reliving that dis-ease.

There is not necessarily anything wrong with re-cycling. When re-cycling without first healing is consciously selected, there may be a desire for further learning about patterns that might have been left. Many of us learn best by repetition, even if this repetition is of undesirable experiences. The truly unfortunate aspect of re-cycling is that the majority of this is done by mistake, without a conscious decision to reexperience a particular cycle for learning purposes.

Of course, the very fact that a being falls back into an old cycle "by mistake" suggests that this being is still tied to the experiences of that cycle. Being tied to an old cycle can be the result of the inability to release attachment to—cording to—patterns, bodies, physical conditions, emotional conditions, peoples, places, things or events within that cycle.

We have discussed extensively problems of attachment in previous volumes and chapters. Here let us simply emphasize the puzzlingly concurrent similarity and distinction between *unwillingly falling back into an old pattern* and *knowingly retaining attachments in order to pull yourself back into the same or a very similar pattern (relationship, addiction, mood swing, economic or disease pattern) you have just left*. Of course, the clue to this puzzle is the word "knowingly." It is quite possible we are unknowingly re-cycling on the surface while knowingly re-cycling all the while.

What do we actually know of what we see ourselves know?

Redescend Consciously

Let's remove physical-plane experience from this model of re-cycling and redescending to further examine it. Once you are conscious of the reality that you are at a *post-death* (or *post-transition) choice point*, that you can choose of your own free will either to ascend out of or to redescend back into old patterns of existence, you can manage to redescend consciously. Or again, as we might better state this: *You can consciously choose to re-descend your consciousness consciously.* If you do decide to journey back "down" and to further explore a cycle you have left, you can manage to learn more in this exploration by planning ahead. In advance of re-cycling:

- Know yourself.
- Know what choice (to or not to redescend or re-cycle) you are making.
- Name clues, markers you want your self to watch for in the event that you become so reinvolved in the old cycle that you forget you are merely returning this time to study yourself there.
- As you redescend, note which cords you reestablish and in what order. Also know that you may not need as many of the old cords this time. A few may be enough to trigger old patterns for "research" purposes.

The more detached you plan to remain as you redescend into an old cycle, the more you can learn there. Also understand that redescension involves becoming more dense again. As you climb down the dimensional ladder, try to remember your experiences in the less dense, more light realms. Remind yourself continuously of what you have seen or perceived "beyond."

Review Pros and Cons

Remain conscious at all times, at all points before, during or even after your redescension into an old cycle of life, an old dimension of your reality. This way you can always opt to cancel the redescension and not further relive the old cycle, even if you feel pressure to do so. One of the positive aspects of *conscious redescension* is that it allows you to take another look at your patterning, your programming. It allows you to move in very close in order to examine the potential for further learning within an old way of being.

The first argument against redescension is that, as noted earlier, this re-cycling is all too often not of one's own free will—or at least the re-cycling is all too often not done consciously. Moreover, the re-cycling event itself can become a habit pattern that is difficult to break. When this happens, beings re-cycle themselves over and over again until they deplete their consciousnesses and wear away their wills. They become trapped in the "no way out" paradox, without enough energy to ever again LEAP into freedom.

It is at this point that absolute death becomes the only escape. This is not dying with grace and power. This is not dying with life beyond. This is surrendering the consciousness to a permanent graveyard of lost and fully diminished will. This is a kind of burnout. This concept applies both to challenging daily-life situations and to the experiences of physical and post-physical death.

Exercise 8.1: Identifying Cycles

Identify five or more cycles, patterns, parts of your life or entire lives that you have experienced or think you have experienced. Call each of these a cycle. Be creative here. Use your imagination if you cannot think of any large or small cycles.

Make a chart similar to the one below. List your cycles, and for each cycle, list the estimated number of times you have already repeated it. Note whether or not you have achieved full mastery of this cycle—whether you have learned all you can learn from it and how many, if any, additional repeats you need to gain full mastery.

Identified Cycle	Number of Repetitions Already Experienced	Has Full Mastery Been Achieved?	Number of Additional Repeats of This Cycle Desired
1.			
2.			
3.			
4.			
5.			
Etc.			

Exercise 8.2: Re-cycling Consciously

Choose one or more of your cycles. Imagine that you make a conscious choice to repeat it, to finally learn all there is to learn from it. What would you do differently this time—now that you have made this conscious choice to learn?

How would you keep yourself conscious of the fact that you have made a conscious choice to repeat this cycle in order to learn from the experience?

Chapter 9

Resurrecting

All this power which is inherent in [the resurrection]—the endowment of life—and which enabled him to rise from the dead, is the very gift of eternal life which he bestows upon the kingdom of believers, and which even now makes certain their resurrection from the bonds of natural death.

—*Paper 190,*
THE URANTIA BOOK

There are many models of overcoming or rising above a challenging situation. Each model involves a profound transitional shift or death. We must allow ourselves to study the possibility that what follows a profound transition is a great adventure, for it is in this post-transition state that we discover so many opportunities, changes, re-formations and new formations of ourselves. Among these states is one that is commonly described as "resurrection." We will discuss resurrection here, not because it is the only avenue of rebundling, the only opportunity for re-forming the self or even the preferred avenue for these, but because it is an important avenue in mythology and in the doctrines of various religions.

The Message of Resurrection

Understand that the concept of resurrection—along with many other concepts essential to consciousness technology—is expressed in mythological and religious literature to open a possibility in the mind that an experience analogous, or similar in some way, can take place. Resurrection is presented in such literature to suggest that resurrection of some sort has indeed actually taken place and therefore that it or something analogous can indeed happen in anyone's reality.

The resurrection of the body—the physical dying and then being reassembled and reconstructed, re-erected—is a message that says that life itself can be rebundled, reformatted after physical death or after movement from one reality or dimension to another. In other words, the dissolution of what are called the body and the self (overlapping and oft seemingly indistinguishable components of one's physical being) is not necessarily the outcome of physical death. The consciousness can live on and, should it choose to, even rebuild itself some sort of matrix. Immortality is indeed possible, say the stories of resurrection.

Resurrection symbolizes rebirth, hope and ascension into a higher state of consciousness. If we think of the challenges and transitions of daily life and the events of life in the traditional "birth to physical death" life cycle, there are many resurrections. There are many major "in life" resurrections, such as: the ordeal of one's birth into infancy, a traumatic divorce, the loss of an important job, a major illness or a disaster. There are even what may be deemed lesser resurrections, such as one following a bout with a moderate flu, when a person stands again, feels whole again, feels comfortable in some way again. This person is resurrected. This person has *made it through*. Even rising up out of bed in the morning after a night's sleep is a resurrection. So the death and resurrection process is something we practice regularly.

Regardless of one's belief system, the notion of resurrection offers a model for understanding transition. One of the most prevalent symbolizations of resurrection is in the biblical story of Christ. As told, Jesus of Nazareth was put to death, crucified, on a large man-made cross and, after burial, was resurrected. This particular "rising from the dead" has been remembered and celebrated for centuries by a large part of Earth's population.

The cross of the *crucifixion of resurrection* is itself an important symbol and a key to other dimensions. That cross symbolizes the intersection of dimensions and the multidimensionality of all existence. It teaches us that (horizontal) reality in the material plane, the third dimension, is intersecting with (vertical) reality beyond, in other dimensions. The cross tells us that death, or the exit from the third dimension, is access to the dimensions beyond and access to what some have decided to call "heaven."

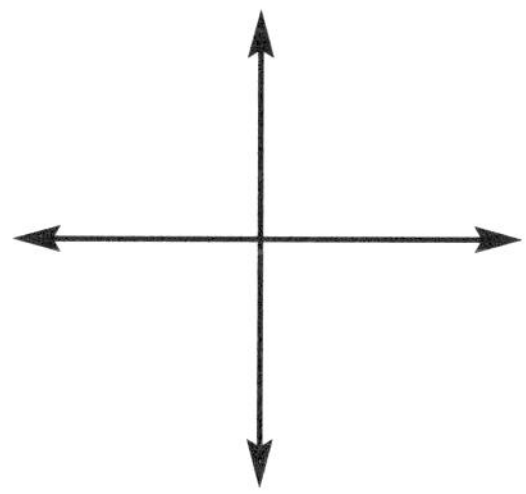

The dimensions beyond the material plane might appear to some to be heaven in that physical suffering may not be possible there. But remember, there are places beyond the physical body where other forms of energy disturbance, tension and knotting—similar to emotional pain, energy conflict and other chaos—may exist. Whether or not we interpret such an energy arrangement as similar to physical pain, there are parallels.

Pain Is a Message

The experience of physical pain can be a message (regarding an energy disturbance or knot)—a message from you to yourself! Perhaps pain is experienced in one form by physical beings living in the third and physical dimension, and conceivably in another form by some physically dead beings who may not have entirely left the third dimension of reality because they have not released their cords. Here, the mythology of resurrection is valuable. This mythology creates the possibility of a complete and clean transition out of this dimension and a complete and clean severance of all cords back to this dimension. A resurrecting of the purified self, even of the healed body or at least of the image of the healed body, symbolizes a liberation from old cords.

Exercise 9.1: Seeing Simple Resurrections

Think of the times in your life when you have resurrected yourself, have come through a challenging physical transition. Try to come up with at least five examples. Include some very simple examples, such as having a fever for a couple of days and feeling absolutely awful, and then feeling very cleansed and pure and relieved when you are well again. Also include some slightly more demanding emotional or physical experiences that you have encountered in your life: diseases, divorces, grievings, addiction recovery processes, traumatic transitions.

Make some notes about these. Describe in a few sentences how your recovery, your transition out of those phases, can be interpreted as a resurrection.

Exercise 9.2: Resurrecting

Whether or not you participate in a religion that believes in resurrection, let us use the imagery of resurrection for this exercise. Keep in mind that we are using imagery to train the mind—to focus, to visualize and to use energy in a particular way that will facilitate the transitional process.

See yourself on an abandoned hill, with no people around. You are on a cross, your arms strung out horizontally on either side of yourself, tied to a horizontal piece of wood that is attached to a vertical piece of wood. Your body is tied to that vertical piece of wood; your feet are tied together at the bottom. Your neck, shoulders and torso are also tied to that vertical piece of wood. You are stretched out on this cross.

You go for days exposed to the weather and without food and water. Eventually your physical body weakens. It can no longer hold you. You, your consciousness, rise out of your physical body. You float higher and higher, expanding as you do. You detach the cords connecting back to your physical body. As you do so, feel the frequency at which you vibrate raise, speed up.

You float even higher above your physical body and continue to look down upon it.

You are still looking down on your body; you are not in any physical state. You access, you feel a light coming to you, a very high, clean vibration of energy. You pull that high vibration into your consciousness. As you do this, you feel yourself pull together. You almost automatically pull your expanding, dispersing consciousness back together to remember and mimic your physical form. As you do, you find the bits of your consciousness reassembling and eventually generating something somewhere like the shape of your physical form.

A major reduction in your vibration now occurs. Like a wave sweeping through you, you shudder. You shrink down from your floating self, but you do not touch the ground. You shrink down, forming this new self, the shape of which appears physical and to be the physical shape you had maintained during the physical life you have just left.

Now you float down and land on the ground in front of your dead, crucified physical body hanging on the cross. Realize that you are not as dense in your resurrected state as you are in your physical state. In your mind's eye, walk the planet this way for a while. Note that only some of the people living in physical bodies see you. Only some eyes see your presence.

After a while, become as dense and physical as the body you began with. Note the reduction in vibration you undergo. Now step out of this story of this cross and back into yourself here and now.

Exercise 9.3: Resurrecting Your Healing

Find yourself again in your body on a cross between dimensions, as at the start of Exercise 9.2. This time the cross is on fire.

Burn, agonize, suffer physically, tremendously. Suffer until your only refuge is to escape your suffering body. Whisk out of that body out of the charring remains of that body.

And now, while outside your damaged physical body, energetically form a nonphysical version of your body, unencumbered by the pain and torture of fire, unfettered by the assault with which it had previously been presented only moments prior. Re-form your body some distance away from the suffering body. Stand in your re-formed body and face it. Stay there awhile. . . . Look.

Now see the burned body heal, return to a healthy state, and climb down from the cross. The healed body now stands before you as you stand before it in the re-formed body you manifested. Guide your re-formed body back into your healed body. Merge with yourself. Try to detect the instant in which the merging is complete. Reenter this dimension.

Chapter 10

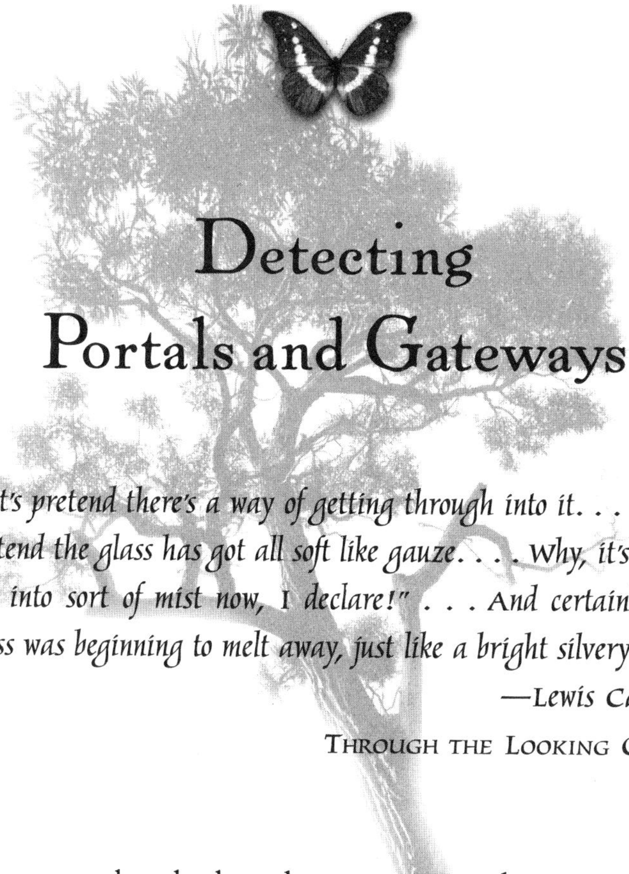

Detecting Portals and Gateways

"Let's pretend there's a way of getting through into it. . . . Let's pretend the glass has got all soft like gauze. . . . Why, it's turning into sort of mist now, I declare!" . . . And certainly the glass was beginning to melt away, just like a bright silvery mist.

—Lewis Carroll,

THROUGH THE LOOKING GLASS

Take a very close look at the air or atmosphere around you. If you relax and do not try too hard to see, you will detect small cracks in this atmosphere. These are pores, windows, *portals*, openings into entirely new realms. Portals are always around you; however, you only see them when you are prepared to do so.

Recognize Portals and Fears of Them

Portals are your gateways into other states of mind, other dimensions of reality, other realms of your consciousness. On your journey through any reality, including the very reality in which you are immersed right now, there will be many portals open to you. Portals are difficult to see from within the physical plane until you learn to recognize them.

Some portals are distinguished as material-plane opportunities—economic, interpersonal, spiritual, philosophical or energetic opportunities. You tend to think of these as life choices. An opportunity may "open up" as a "way out" of a troubled cycle you are trapped in. You do not take that opportunity, you do not travel through such a portal:

- if you are too attached to the troubled or heavily corded cycle you are in
- if you are afraid of change
- if you are afraid of dying and you realize that you must die out of your old behavior or cycle to move through a portal
- if you do not know how to see the portal for what it is
- if you do not feel confident in your ability to evaluate such a portal

Evaluate Portals

Whether or not your portals present themselves as physical-plane life opportunities or as non-material energy formations similar to windows in the atmosphere, you can use your mind's eye to evaluate them:

- A portal is sometimes found behind a clutter of energies of varying degrees of light. Look deeply to see (as in Figure 10.1). Sometimes a portal comes into focus once one's gaze is trained (as in Figure 10.2).
- For a portal to offer a way to a higher, more conscious

opportunity, it must have more light coming out of it than your current environment holds [see Figure 10.3].

- When a portal offers light of the same or a lesser quality than the light of your present atmosphere, do not travel through it.
- Look before LEAPing. Gaze into the core of the portal, into the center of its opening. Do not force yourself to focus or to be hypnotized. Just gaze consciously.
- If eventually your gaze reveals a vehicle of transport (such as in Figure 10.4), then know that this vehicle does not fly you somewhere against your will. This vehicle only travels where the free will of your consciousness sends it. Your consciousness both powers and directs your vehicle. Your consciousness even constructs your vehicle. Your consciousness *is* your vehicle.
- So long as the light of the portal is pure and clear, and so long as you feel no compulsion, suction or hypnotic suggestion to enter, you know that this is a safe portal.
- Look for portals that meet the above criteria and that, upon close examination, reveal portals within portals within them—each portal containing the precious vehicle you can drive with your own consciousness, and each portal exuding a purer light than the one preceding or surrounding it [see Figure 10.5]. These are portals of escalated ascension, infinite portal transports into the ever higher realms of energy and light.
- Remember, any suction or hypnotization you feel is a sign that you are being deceived, pulled in, without the agreement of your own free will.
- Always be ready to turn away from the pull of an illusion!

Figure 10.1. Light amidst disorientation.

Figure 10.2. Opening in the atmosphere.

Figure 10.3. An opening to light.

Figure 10.4. Vehicle of transport entering the portal vortex.

Figure 10.5. Repeating infinite portal vortex with vehicles of transport.

Registering Rainbows of Light

Pure white Light is comprised of all the colors of light—let's say the purest of each of the seven colors, "rays" or frequencies of light. There will be times during your journey of consciousness into what lies beyond physical reality when the Light will register itself to you this way, as a perfect rainbow of seven perfect rays. A seven-rayed light prism may occur at special portals, gateways, to the purest, whitest Light. Allow your consciousness to construct this prism with what you may presently call your imagination. Basically this prism is a concept, an idea, an invocation of energies in a certain balance, a complete balance, which represents all light combined.

See, imagine seeing, the rainbow as the message, as the instruction, as the path or stairway to complete, whole Light. You can travel through the "rainbow realm," over the "rainbow bridge," into the Light by moving from the lowest frequency up to the highest frequency of color, merging all frequencies, until you resonate at a high enough frequency that it will be but a small step into the complete white Light.

If and when you encounter a rainbow bridge or portal, use the colors as stepping stones. Start vibrating low like red, then up to orange, then yellow, then green, then blue, then indigo, then violet. As you step up, pull each of the lower color vibrations with you, as if you are collecting them. You are not shifting frequencies upward; you are combing them from low to high until you are at full-spectrum white Light. The sum of the rays is far greater than all of its seven parts. It is the purest Light.

Know Gateways to Greater Free Will

Know what forms white Light. Be able to dissect light you see into a rainbow to see whether it is a true rainbow, a true representation of all light, whole Light. The matter of avoiding the lure of false Light will always be with you. A consciousness such as yours desires this survival skill. There are times when darkness disguises itself as Light. Everyone is subject to being deceived.

Your own trained discernment is the most sure protection. If you are sucked into a portal *posing itself* to be one of those pictured in Figures 10.2 and 10.3, you may not be ascending, nor may you be moving in the direction of increasing free will. Such *suction gates*, dressed as gateways to the higher realms of Light, suck on, deplete your will. (As your free will and your own consciousness erode away, a *vacuum of vulnerability* is left inside your soul. This is when you are open to being kidnapped, trapped, enslaved. You are responsible for avoiding this event.)

Do not relinquish the freedom of your own responsibility. Do not allow a false Light to program you. Programmed people are consciousnesses that are not free, yet they are energy-production robots. Whatever bit of free consciousness nestled within those consciousnesses that have been kidnapped and turned to robots, is trapped, caged, suffocating. Too many beings needlessly allow themselves to be trapped this way.

What you do here, in your present—and in your case, physical—dimension, has effects far beyond the reality you see and know. Look for ways to override your programming and patterning. *Patterns, whatever their symptoms, trap energy.* Be careful how you use your energy in the here and now, whether it is your physical, your emotional, your financial or your spiritual energy. Try to see the patterns you are forming and feeding. Try to see the choices you make. Try to evaluate the lights to which you are attracted.

TRY TO DISCOVER WHETHER THE THOUGHTS YOU ARE THINKING ARE YOUR OWN.

Remember that entering a portal into a new reality is a form of transition, a shift, a death. Will you commit to selecting only the portals that are gateways to increasing free will? Freedom fighters die for liberty—will you find out what this means? Will you undergo the shift involved here?

You will know when you arrive at the threshold of conscious liberty, of freedom of consciousness. Until you know, wait. Wait, wait on, because you have time. Time is what you have—time and your own essence.

Exercise 10.1: Seeing Openings and Comparing Portals

Right now, with your eyes open, pretend that you see openings that look to be very, very large, filmy entries at various locations in your environment, in the atmosphere around you—like mouths of caves covered with a translucent substance. These filmy areas can appear to be indented, as if they are convex eyes or bubbles curving away from you like lenses. Realize that each of these is the opening to another realm or a passage, a walkway— a passage into another realm.

Now close your eyes and imagine that you see many, many, many more of these portals. You realize that each of them has a slightly different characteristic, a slightly different light coming from it, a slightly different magnetic pull on you, a slightly different degree of and type of interest in you or attraction to you, a slightly different vibration.

Begin to think about the possible differences in experience you would have should you choose to sample the crossing of the membranes into each of these portals and the space beyond these membranes.

Come back.

Exercise 10.2: Feeling Portals

Close your eyes, right here where you sit or stand right now. With both your hands, reach before you into the air or atmosphere and begin to feel the space in front of you with your fingertips. Imagine that—or actually notice that—the atmosphere you are touching has great variations in energy and density. Sometimes these variations are within an inch of each other or within a foot of each other or within a few feet or further apart.

Notice that you can feel what your fingertips touch, as well as what your fingertips perceive to be out in front of them, some distance away.

Where you find significant differences in the atmosphere, begin to use your hands to detect the presence of a portal, an opening to another dimension. When you think you have found one, stay with it. Or if you do not think you have found one, just use your imagination, invent a portal, and stay with it.

Use your fingertips to feel the edges of that portal. Feel all the way around it, and then use your fingertips to feel the membrane of that portal's opening. Feel it very gently, delicately, as if you don't want to pop the membrane. Although this membrane appears thin and filmy and weak, it is very strong and very selective as to what it lets through. Still, treat it gingerly and with great respect.

Hold for the next exercise. Stay with this portal.

Exercise 10.3: Responding Consciously to the Opportunity Offered by a Portal

Bow, bend over or nod your head downward, as if you are nodding or bowing in respect before this portal. See the portal as the mouth of an energy greater than yours. As you bow, check inside to be sure you feel that this portal deserves your respect, your awe.

Ask yourself or ask this portal (or both): Is this a benign, a patent-

ly divine presence, or is this an illusion, a dark space wearing the mask of light, a suction seeking to kidnap the energy you have generated by your consciousness, seeking to suck you in and take you over?

If you have hesitation while bowing, cease bowing in respect. Come back to face the portal and say, "No, thank you, not today. I choose to go another way." If, on the other hand, you do choose to feel with great awe and respect this divinely potent energy (this door to this divinely potent energy that this portal represents), complete your bow and request permission to enter by stating, "I request permission of my own free will."

Stop. Come back.

Chapter 11

Passing GO: Vehicles of Transport

The impression of inertia is due to the powerful spans of energy that must be crossed within seconds of flight. . . . In order to overcome high-frequency resistance levels, it is necessary to go beyond compound matter-energy "bondings" which are contained within electromagnetic "skins" and are impenetrable by the lower physical intelligence.

—J. J. Hurtak,
The Book of Knowledge: The Keys of Enoch

You are now a long, long way into your brave adventures in conscious transitioning and shifting. And still there is more to discover. Now it is time to pass GO, with full speed ahead.

As you move from one dimension of reality to another, from one format of your existence to another, you approach and then eventually pass a key point in your journey: GO. [See Figures 11.1 and 11.2.] Whether you come to this point called GO after you consciously choose to enter a particular opportunity—a gateway or portal—or after you fall or are sucked into it, is of course

Figure 11.1. Approaching GO.

Figure 11.2. In GO.

up to you. As we have explained, the level of awareness you bring to such a journey—to the traversing of realities, of dimensions, of formats—has great bearing on how you come to this point called GO. Passing GO is passing a marker (or marking the concept that a marker has been passed)—the point of rebundling and re-creating the self and moving on as the old highly corded lower-body self is now less probable, likely not possible.

Pay Attention at GO

Pay attention here at GO. Once you pass GO, turning back can feel very difficult. Once past GO, to return to the place from which you just came, to move backward, you may have to unbundle the self you have already rebundled. You have to undo, reverse your dance of creation. You have to dissolve the new matrix you have already begun to manifest. You have to move again through the processes we have discussed in the previous chapters, this time in reverse. And you can do this if you choose. However, once past GO, the increased momentum deeper into the beyond makes it difficult to turn back.

We do not call GO the "point of no return," because as we note in the next chapter, many do choose to return, although they usually do not return in a form very like the one they have just left. As elusive as this concept "the point called GO" is, this is indeed a key concept, moment and location within the transitioning consciousness.

When you pass this GO point, you will know. You will feel as if you have pulled yourself back together after dissolving to get through a membrane. You will feel that the membrane you have moved through or crossed over is a one-way membrane. However, this is not really a one-way membrane; it only appears as such. The work of crossing back through this membrane, if you stay conscious, *can* be done. This "work" or endeavor can even be fascinating and challenging.

At GO, it is most important for you to look back and appreciate your passage through the membrane, to savor the experience you have just had of successfully moving through this semipermeable membrane, this membrane that only allows purified essences to pass through. In that All That Is is both perceived and defined by your consciousness as existing, even the membrane you pass through and the point of GO are constructs of your consciousness.

Transport Consciousness Beyond

Consciously passing GO and then to the realms beyond GO involves the transport of your consciousness in a special way. You can learn to transport your consciousness in a vehicle that your consciousness constructs out of energy and light. This is the vehicle of transport described in Figure 11.2, which is comprised of two triangular light-energy structures that form a diamondlike arrangement. Study the details of Figure 11.2.

To operate this light-energy vehicle and to ride this vehicle into the beyond, study the practices described in Exercises 11.1, 11.2, 11.3 and 11.4. These exercises describe the entering of the light vehicle and offer images (and concepts) designed to get this vehicle to move, to spin and to allow you to travel while (and from) within it.

Exercise 11.1: Entering the Vehicle of Transport

Visualize the figure in Figure 11.3. See the two triangles as balanced in such a way that the space between them is presently horizontal.

Figure 11.3. Vehicle of transport.

Imagine yourself climbing into this horizontal space as if it were a ship. The walls of the ship are made of energy that appears to be light. You can get into the space defined by those walls by climbing into the horizontal space between them and sitting there. Sit within that horizontal space and hold for the next exercise.

Exercise 11.2: Triggering Movement of the Vehicle of Transport

Realize how stable this vehicle of energy in the form of light is while in the horizontal resting position. Hang on to this concept of stabilization, as you can always call this to you to stabilize your energy.

Now imagine that someone has this vehicle of light balanced at the top of a hill like a rock. Gently but nevertheless forcibly, this vehicle is being pushed down the hill. It rolls. Feel yourself roll, still in that central control-room area—which was horizontal but now is not—as the vehicle tumbles down the hill. Continue tumbling, stay in this tumble, and feel how the energy changes as you roll in that space between the two triangles. Continue this as you hold for the next exercise.

Exercise 11.3: Flying the Vehicle of Transport

The hill continues. You are rolling downward. At a certain point, you realize that each time that space between the two triangles of the light vehicle is pointing at least somewhat vertically toward the sky (or what you consider to be an upward direction), you feel energy sweep through you. Decide that on one of these tumbles, when you are pointing in an almost vertical direction, you will use that energy that sweeps up through you and your vehicle to propel the vehicle upward so that you do not have to finish the downhill roll.

Here you come. You are now in the position that points vertically. The energy sweeps through you and the vehicle of transport. You fill yourself with intent to move upward.

Fly off the hill, and then once off the hill, continue tumbling, rolling round and round in what you consider to be a generally upward direction. Fly further upward, still tumbling. You have shifted the direction of your vehicle's motion by using the energy moved and released when the space between the triangles was vertical. Hold for the next exercise as you continue shunting upward in an energetic tumble.

Exercise 11.4: Flying into Higher Realms

Now imagine that you are tumbling, not just through your material-plane atmosphere, but into other realms of density, less and less dense and more and more light. See in the distance a beautiful realm, full of very, very bright light. Aim your intent in that direction.

The next moment in which you again find your vehicle of light balancing its control room in what you feel to be an upward or vertical direction and its energy sweeps upward through you, aim yourself, aim your intent, to the beautiful realm you have selected. Imagine that you tumble very quickly toward this realm.

You find yourself in this next realm. The space between the triangles of your vehicle is now horizontal; you are stabilized. You pause there.

You will stay there as long as you choose. This is your vehicle; you can use it for transport. This is you. The vehicle works better when you purposefully begin to spin instead of getting pushed down a hill as if you were a top or the vehicle were a top. Begin this spin of your own accord—having your consciousness create and then drive this vehicle—instead of using (perceived) gravity to set it off. Experiment awhile, and then return to Earth or your starting dimension.

An examination of Figures 11.4 and 11.5 will reveal the vehicle's technology—the cyclical movement from the destabilization of death into the spinning climb of ascension, into the restabilization of liberation, all made conscious by knowing the operation of the light-energy vehicle. This is a consciousness technology you will remember long after death and use in many dimensions.

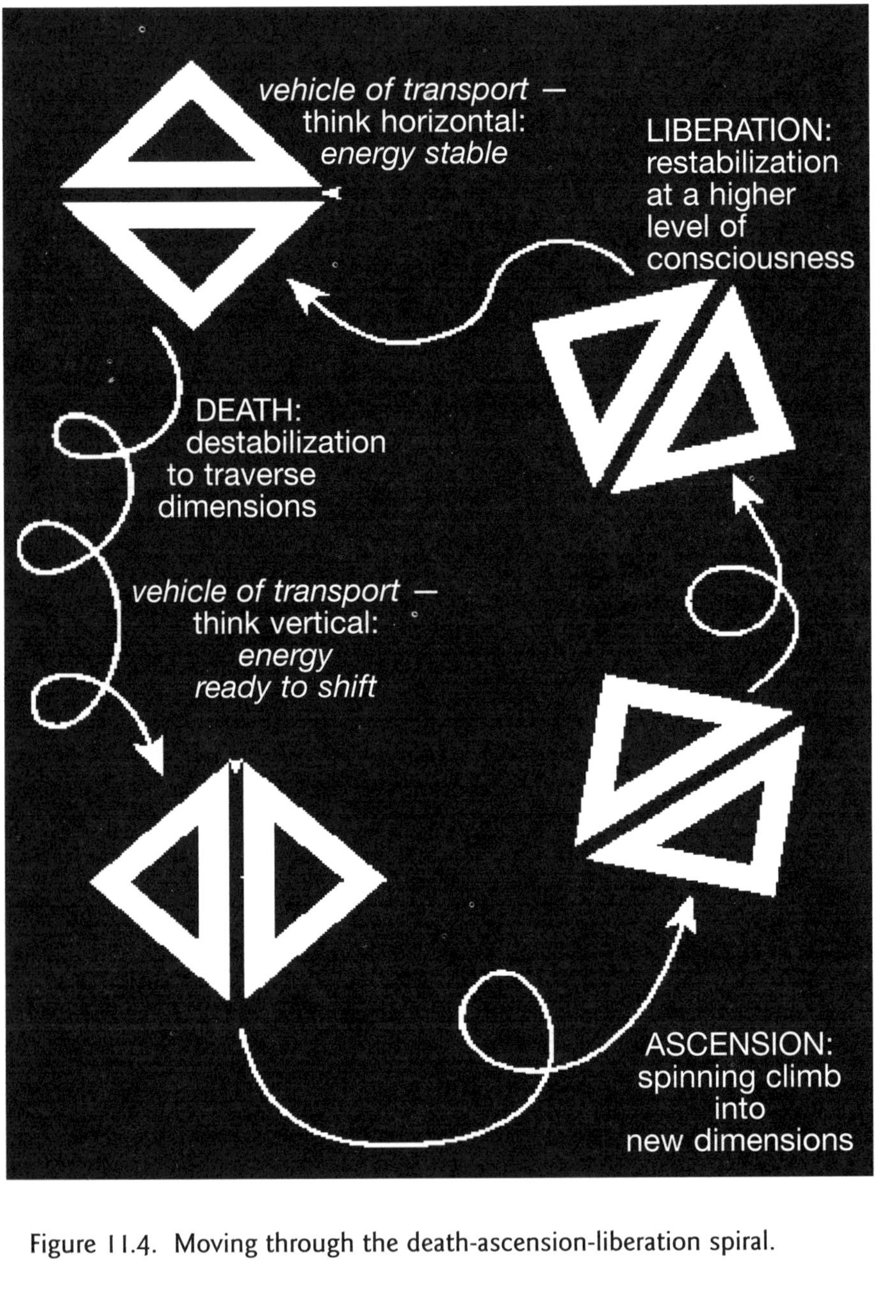

Figure 11.4. Moving through the death-ascension-liberation spiral.

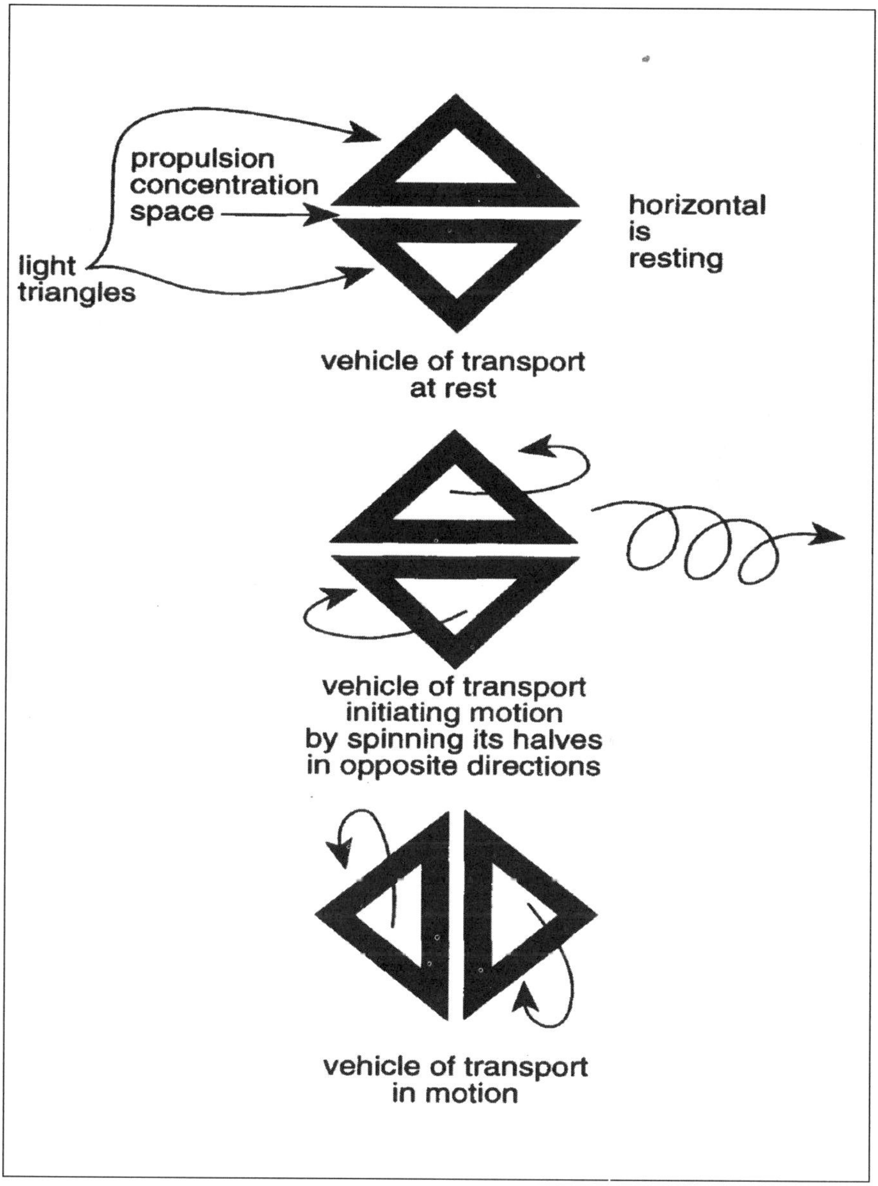

Figure 11.5. Operating instructions for vehicle of transport.

Chapter 12

Delivering Oneself into Another Dimension

I fled the earth and, naked, climbed the weather,
Reaching a second ground far from the stars.

—Dylan Thomas,
"I Fellowed Sleep"

There comes a time to go. Deep inside we know when this is. When we fully release, entirely reject our attachments, *when we liberate ourselves from our attachments to worldly experiences* such as friendships, feelings, foods, music, art, business, pain and suffering, we free our attention to focus upon something far more subtle, far more abstract, far more real than so-called "worldly" experiences. Once we are fully liberated, a new kind of understanding or vision of truth can come to us. We can then see ourselves as something other and far more than what we had seen ourselves as being.

Know the Potential of Eternal Consciousness

Even before detaching, it is valuable to focus on this notion of the cosmic self, on your consciousness's potential of becoming eternal, of *defining itself as eternal.* Such a focus trains the consciousness to utilize energies to know itself and to fuel itself. That your consciousness is who you really are—that you are not your body, not your house, not who people say you are, not who you may tell yourself you are in terms of your surface characteristics and feelings, not your material-plane identity—is a larger realization than it may at first seem.

Wrapping your mind around the largeness, the expansiveness of your existence is a lot. Coming to terms with who you are, getting to know who you really are, is a big step in the evolution of your consciousness. This is when your consciousness realizes on a deep level that all it surrounds itself with in the material plane is not itself. This is when your consciousness meets itself, wakes up to its identity.

Focus on Energies That Can Fuel Consciousness

Focus on the energies coming in to you from the cosmic whole. By doing this, you can move the energy you find nourishing up and down and through your body to achieve high states of what some would describe (from the perspective of their human existence) as bliss, love and ecstasy. Realize that these are but weak emotions when attached to material reality.

This is not to say that your basic experiences in the attachment-prone physical world are valueless. The experiences that you collect and undergo in the physical dimension are excellent training for your travels beyond this dimension, into your consciousness and the world it defines. Therefore, it is not suggested that you suppress material-plane emotion and attachment. Instead, harness the energy you cultivate and hold in these attachments. Harness the energy and then release it at a time when release is useful in the strengthening of your consciousness. Do this with care, to perform the LEAPs in consciousness we discuss in this volume. These LEAPs are *expansions of you*—of your consciousness.

Although your involvement in third-dimensional experience is not in any way entirely negative or unnecessary, an enslavement to such involvement, a sort of automatic addictive drive to maintain and continue such involvement, is a problem. Simply stated, your addiction to your addictions and to your reality itself can drain you, perhaps disable or even kill who you really are, drain and even kill your consciousness.

If you tie yourself to a ship, it floats but holds you down and you stagnate. If your ship sinks and you remain tied to it, you not only stagnate but go down with it. Stagnation winds down your energy. Stagnation drains and kills energy. Remember, by "you" we mean your consciousness. A rigid addiction to your reality stifles the flow of your energy, energy that you could be using to generate the ascent into new strength and new realms of your own consciousness.

Exercise 12.1: Designing One's Delivery Beyond

Reread the last exercise in the previous chapter. What did you do there? You delivered yourself into another dimension. As noted in previous chapters, there are many methods of doing this. Combine these methods or keep them separate. Your delivery of yourself into another dimension is your own process. You will develop and refine your own consciousness technology tools.

Your assignment now is to fashion a delivery of yourself into another dimension. You may want to consult the following exercis-

es, as well as the exercises that you have already completed, to put together some series of activities or thought processes designed to deliver "you" into another dimension. Or you might want to pick one of the exercises and add to it. Or you may want to write your own death and ascension technology.

However you choose to do it, your assignment here is to plan and practice your chosen LEAP into another dimension of your choice. Keep in mind that exercising free will in the preservation and further development of your consciousness is key to surviving most consciously.

Exercise 12.2: Delivering Oneself Beyond

Now practice several times your self-designed delivery of your self-designed self into another dimension of reality. With each practice, amend your method of deliverance to increase its degree of believability for you. Note what changes you choose to make and why.

Note where your imagination empowers your consciousness.

Chapter 13

Merging—But with What?

For, if energy can be released by the disintegration of matter—this is the most common method—it can also be released by fusion.

—*Omraam Mikhaël Aïvanhov,*
FRUITS OF THE TREE OF LIFE:
THE CABBALISTIC TRADITION

As you merge (should you decide to do so), think of this merging as both a surrender and an intercourse. This is a surrender because you are giving up—either momentarily or for good—your sovereignty, your independent free will, in this merge. This is an intercourse because it is a union. You become one with that with which you merge by meshing energies.

Surrender Consciously

At this advanced stage of your journey into the beyond, this merging and intercourse act is most likely to be engaging you with something much less dense, far more expansive and powerful, and intensely lighter than yourself. This can be the pinnacle of one's experience; however, this must be understood to be embraced.

A temporary or permanent, partial or complete giving over of your self, your consciousness, to this something is not necessarily an undesirable experience. This can be the most exhilarating of all your experiences. However, a giving over of your self, without determining carefully what you are giving your self over to and to what degree, can be dangerous. Hence, when you are about to merge, pause and ask what it is you are merging with—and who you are when you merge.

Merge consciously. You can use the various methods of discernment previously discussed, applying your analysis of the light to the light/energy body, consciousness or intelligence with which you are preparing to merge. A conscious understanding of the intercourse that takes place when you merge is important.

Know Intercourse Tantra

You are about to mesh energies, to make a trade or exchange at a very high and very stripped-down, naked level. Are you prepared? Such high-level exchange is an *integrative tantra.* You can begin to train for this form of tantra while still in a physical body. As you merge with anyone or any energy, understand that you are having intercourse with a force outside your own.

When you merge with an energy body, maintain your awareness during your intercourse with this energy body, foreign intelligence (not part of you), life form or energy mass. This can be the highest union possible, or it can be the highest union that a somewhat inexperienced being has yet to encounter. Teach yourself now, while you are still in a physical body, that all that glitters is not gold. Attractions (even sexual or romantic) can be quite deceptive. You know this from your physical-plane experience. Prepare to take this knowledge out to the realms of immaterial energies.

Once outside your body, you will want to be able to understand the profound tantra of an intercourse with light. Study now, while still in physicality, the Eastern traditions of tantra, a practice that maps the subtle emotional or nonphysical body, collects energy at various points in the subtle body, and then moves those energies in a way that seeks to elevate the consciousness.

Sexual tantra between physical partners is the exchange of harnessed, collected and moved energies from one body to another and back, forming a circuit of energy and thus a merging of energy. Of course, when this practice is carried beyond the physical plane, you may find you intercourse with a far more expansive energy mass than another physical body. We speak of "intercourse" in order to inject a greater degree of consciousness into the merging interaction, greater than simple surrender. "Surrender" tends to be a less conscious interaction with the energy mass than "intercourse."

When you are less conscious than the energy with which you are intercoursing, you allow the energy mass greater discernment than you have and thus more power. And once you are past the point of your surrender, you are left with no discernment, no power. (When another energy entirely dominates a union to the point that there is no free will being exercised by the partner energy in the union, an energetic parallel to rape can take place.)

Although there is always a degree of surrender in the act of intercourse, the surrendering body or bodies can always retain awareness and participate consciously in the intercourse interaction, the merging and the later separations (if the merging is not final) of their energies. Intercourse, if done in a highly aware state, allows you to know and feel the energy with which you intend to merge and then decide how long or how completely to merge with this energy.

You may know this based upon your experience with physical sex. However, *what we speak of here can far surpass physical sex in intensity and in significance.* Understand that we are in no way negating the value of the material reality in which you presently find yourself. We do not call for your denial of the reality of physical life or physical sex. What we do call for is your understanding that physical-plane experience is only a place on a broader multidimensional spectrum. When you understand this, then your realization that you are part of a greater system—a larger, frequently nonmaterial, cosmic whole—makes merging a completely different process.

Use Intuition in Merging

See merging not as a once-in-a-lifetime event, so to speak, but as a chain of events that is at work again and again at the same or on the more dense or less dense, more concrete or less tangible, levels of reality. It is better to see any potential energy intercourse or merging as an opportunity with which you are presented, as one in a series of opportunities coming to you in your journey through the cosmos of your expansive reality.

So long as you treat merging as more of a conscious intercourse than a blind surrender, you can explore a series of opportunities to merge as part of your long ascent. Always, you must exercise discernment. Turn down some mergings. Intercourse momentarily with others, but withhold the core of your consciousness in order to be able to separate after you have exchanged information with the energy mass. Enjoy prolonged intercourse with but one or a few energies clear enough and pure enough to elevate you (or for you to mutually elevate). Emerge from all these mergings until you are ready (if you ever eventually wish) to choose consciously to merge for good.

Be careful: You are creating something when you merge. Each merging is a creation. It creates an effect, a result, an energy offspring of the exchange. Some will call this a new birth; others will say this is a rebirth. Some will call this a genesis, or even a healing. You want to be certain that your consciousness is giving birth to an energy form it desires to proliferate. Do not intercourse with an energy with whom you would not like to create an offspring energy.

Exercise 13.1: Examine the Energy That Beckons Your Merge

Reread the exercises (in the previous volumes and chapters of this volume) that address initiating, identifying and clarifying the light. Now write your own procedure for determining the nature of a very large, very powerful energy form that you encounter outside of the physical plane. Use a step-by-step approach, and do write this one out on paper if you can.

Exercise 13.2: Testing Your Discernment

Now you will apply your method of examination—you will discern the nature of an energy form that has no characteristics you can see with your physical eyes.

Close your eyes. Imagine or actually locate a very large nonphysical energy mass. (This mass may or may not be connected to a physical body.) With your consciousness, approach this mass, but do not merge with it. Discern the nature of this mass by applying the steps you put together for yourself in Exercise 13.1. Revise your steps if need be. Write down your revisions if possible.

Figure 13.1. The value of discerning what is out there.

Chapter 14

Ascending: LEAP Level Five

I have beheld with the all-seeing eyes of mind the unseen things . . . and as I examined them, there came to me by slow degrees, but came in very deed, accurate knowledge of the truth.

—Hermes Trismegistus
to his son Tat,
HERMETICA

Take a moment to fix your higher sight beyond all that you know, all that you take for granted. Look beyond—beyond what you know as your daily life, your accepted reality, beyond your physical existence, your physical health, your physical sense of self.

You have sensed what is beyond so many times. You have sensed this, even glimpsed it, but can you find the energy to travel all the way there? Can you ascend to these high realms of being, of energy and light? Yes, you *can* ascend to the portals of whatever realms of reality you choose to perceive as existing. Your consciousness perceives these realms in whatever form it prefers. At each portal to each realm, you can clarify and purify to cross over the membrane. And once you cross over, you can choose to ascend again to the next level.

Learn Kundalini Death

What we will herein call *kundalini death* is the process of using the energy flow within your physical body—or parallel to what you would have in your physical body—as fuel providing the power to launch. All of the physical-body activities, including sex, are training in the technical aspects of using energy, or what is sometimes called "kundalini."

Many so-called Western teachings have emphasized the sexual aspects of the Eastern traditions regarding kundalini. Yet kundalini is much more than what is typically learned (and oft even misunderstood) in the physical plane. In fact, sexual energy itself is so much more than that generated between physical beings who are physically attracted to each other.

Feel Death's Sexuality

Kundalini is a "yoga"—an exercise that involves the stretching, relaxing and invigorating of the consciousness to heighten its awareness and help it access other dimensions of reality. Kundalini "sex," as taught in the physical plane, involves the control of one's breathing and the focus of one's mental energy such that the energy generated by a sexual meditation, stimulation and interaction can be moved up and down the spine or vertical axis. Here, what we will call kundalini death moves, even propels energy up the spine and then right out the top of the head to help you leave your body and travel to realms far, far from your present energy dimension.

Exercise 14.1: Moving Sexual Energy

Earlier volumes and exercises have discussed the movement of energy up and down the spine or vertical axis. Imagine that such energy is now moving up and down your spine. Do this for a few minutes.

Now continue this energy-moving process, but first generate some of what we will here describe as "sexual" energy in yourself. Remember that sexual energy can be experienced anywhere in your emotional or physical body and is not restricted to your sex organs or to interaction with another person. We include physical stimulation here, as this is the most commonly recognized avenue of sexual arousal in physically incarnated humans. Ways of generating sexual energy in yourself include:

- *Simply imagine that you are sexually aroused.*
- *If you are alone or with a partner with whom you are sexually intimate, excite yourself or have your partner excite you physically.*
- *Excite your physical sexuality by imaging or fantasizing what you think of as a sexy encounter.*
- *Recall the experience of physical orgasm and attempt to replicate the sensations leading up to this experience with no physical stimulation or sexual fantasy.*

If you are unsuccessful in generating some sexual energy within yourself, simply imagine that you have generated some sexual energy. Just imagine or create the signs or symptoms of this energy, whatever those signs may be for you. Suggested symptoms or signs this sexual energy might include are:

- *physical arousal*

- *raised frequency of heartbeat and breathing*
- *raised body temperature*
- *a general sense of physical and emotional excitement and anticipation*
- *a feeling of internal fire or glow, feeling like warm pleasure*

Now take this anticipatory, exciting, pleasurable energy and put it at the base of your spine. Focus on its presence there. Proceed to move the sexual energy up your vertical axis (spine), continuing through this exercise much more rapidly now. When you get this sexual energy to the top of your head, reverse the exercise, moving the energy step by step back down your spine.

Run this energy from the base of your spine to the top of your head and back down and up again many times. Start to feel exhilarated as you do this. Start to feel as though there is an electrical energy shooting up and down your spine. Continue doing this into the next exercise.

Exercise 14.2: Using Sexual Energy as Fuel for LEAPing

As you make this energy more and more powerful by running it up and down your spine again, again and again, prepare your mind for your launch into energetic ascension. Continue moving the energy up and down your spine. As you do so, think but do not yet do . . . think about what it will be like to shoot this energy (you) out the top of your head. Think about how it will be to shoot your energy so far away from your body that it LEAPs across many realms of density, energy and light into a very, very, very expanded, vaporous, brightly lit realm.

Keep moving your sexual energy up and down your spine. Get ready . . . you are going to let the energy burst out the top of your head.

Up and down your spine, then up, up and up out the top of your head—and you LEAP into the Light! Ascend into the Light!

Ascend Consciously

Energy can fuel ascension. *Conscious ascension* is simply a purposeful harnessing of energy to fuel a shifting to a new perception of reality and a new arrangement of the energy within reality. Ascension is the conscious lifting of a pattern of behavior, emotion, health or physical energy in such a manner that it ascends or climbs into a higher, less-dense arrangement of energy—a higher, less-dense frequency of sound and light, a higher realm of one's own consciousness—then works with the less-dense energy matrix from that locus where the energy is more malleable, and then resets the shifted energy pattern or structure back into the reality from which it came. Healing takes place. Conscious shift construction takes place, bringing about the healing of patterns and matrices.

What you have come to know in physicality as sexual energy can be transformed to so much more. The tantric kundalini death LEAP you are asked to practice above fuels conscious, aware, discerning ascension. Recognize that the energy and consciousness you bring to your ascension determines its outcome.

With any intimate discussion of death being a taboo in many social circles, this sort of discussion of sexuality (which is also a taboo in many social circles)—the actual energetic form of the *sexuality of conscious dying*—must be handled delicately. The basic message here is that sexual energy is much more than the untrained physical body may see, and that sexual energy can fuel an efficient, profound and stimulating shift. Sexual energy is only physically sexual for those who either choose to reduce it to physical-sexual density or who as of yet know of no similar parallel form of ecstatic, transformative energy.

An expanded awareness of the dimensions of reality beyond the physical plane changes a being's understanding of all energy, including sexual energy, and of all vehicles of personal change, healing and reality-shifting. As energy drives these vehicles of change, transition, healing and reality-shifting, mastery of non-physical sexual energy can enhance all change, transition, healing and reality-shifting, including the death transition—which, in truth, all transitions, all endings and beginnings, are.

PART III

How to Discern and Cathart Out of an Existing Emotional or Physical Condition or Reality

Part III of this volume takes the consciousness further on this journey of the imagination and of the will, allowing the consciousness to strengthen itself and its awareness in preparation for conscious transitioning, changing, shifting, healing and survival. The "in daily life" and "in end of life" relevances of this ever-developing metaphorical depiction of change, transition, healing and death further elaborates itself here.

Chapter 15

Discerning What Beckons

Be willing to change the timing or form of your holy understanding of Truth so as to climb the octaves of Jacob's Ladder through initiations of refinement.

—*22nd Commandment,*
VIRTUES, LAWS AND POWERS

Any port in a storm? No! Where we take ourselves, our essences, matters. Assessing the pathways, openings and portals to new states of health, balance, mind and body—realities—requires conscious attention.

Discernment is careful examination and valuing. Discernment is the determination of the degree, quality and clarity of the opportunity, essence, energy and/or light with which we are being presented. Without understanding discernment, you are subjected to whatever influences come your way. You arc at risk of bringing in—accepting as they come in, allowing in or actually making welcome—forces, intelligences and energy bodies that may or may not have the best interests of your existence, of humanity or of humanity's evolution at heart.

As you read this chapter on discernment, recognize that you can apply this information, with slight translation, to the use of your consciousness and intelligence during your everyday life in your material plane, including in adapting and healing processes. Here we focus primarily on interdimensional shifting as it is triggered by physical death. However, all this is also a metaphor for everyday life, which is loaded with shifts, even dimensional shifts. Thus every iota of this material is a metaphor for all your changes and transitions, large and small.

Refine Discernment

"Just go for the light" is the advice some people give each other. However, wise, aware discernment is more delicate than this. After all, if "darkness" were coming in, wouldn't it be apt to disguise itself as "light"? Many debates rage over definitions of Light with a capital "L."

Frequently, these disagreements are cloaked in the veil of religious debate. What typically happens is that if the true "Light" of one person doesn't match up with the true "Light" of another, and yet they both feel that they are talking about the true, true, truest of Light, then they may denounce each other's Light. This is no way to make such a precious judgment, and this is not discernment. There are many handles on the pot of Light being talked about. Light—highest purest Light—is a concept of purity, in some worldviews of divinity, which can be shared while being labeled differently by the various people appreciating this concept.

Especially in times of great change and transition, times such as your now, you must be adept at keeping your own *keenly alert counsel.* Only then can you effectively evaluate what beckons you once you are leaving and/or have left your old condition or reality. To a great extent, we do create our own personal realities. To a great extent, we do create the realities we transition into. This is because our abilities to perceive and then to label our perceptions are so powerful. This does not mean we should blame ourselves for all that is less than desirable about our lives and selves. After all, our environments have a great deal of influence upon us. Still, our definitions of, interactions with and effects upon our environments can be up to us.

To a great extent, we are all involved in evolving the overall cosmic reality. Discernment is one of our tools of personal and species evolution. Thus, as you move through realities, especially through death transitions, as refined a discernment process as *you* can manifest is valuable for you and for all of us.

Refined discernment is not only valuable, it is essential. If you are not sufficiently discerning, what comes in to this and other dimensions through you—into the space you inhabit—can affect the energy of the life forms, of those people around you, not just of you. When you work hard to learn to open yourself up to multidimensional awareness and consciousness but fail to learn discernment, you are a risk factor for everyone.

You can open wide up like a big leak in a reservoir wall and allow troubled mindsets and energy—what is oft called "darkness," dangerous factors—to pour in by not discerning as you open up. You can allow undesirable forces, energies and life forms to pour right into your material plane, through you. *So your ability to discern is of critical importance to more than just you. This ability to discern can contribute to the positive evolution of the consciousness when discerningly utilized.*

Discernment Is a Right and a Responsibility

Discernment is therefore both a right and a responsibility. This discernment must be continuous and not only implemented during the peak of a living or physical-death transition, when you are perhaps more vulnerable. This is because there are always fluctuations in your degree of vulnerability to energies coming in. And you are always undergoing various forms of transitions, cycle-closings and deaths, many less obvious to you than others but equally critical. Therefore, continuously discerning is valuable.

Discernment is a serious matter. Your discernment helps protect the life force and the soul of humanity from being waned and even subsumed. This being subsumed is also a death, but not the potential-laden, even potentially energy-building transitional death we have been focusing on. Most forms of death are absolutely not absolute death, but absolute death is absolute death. This absolute death is a difficult death to see. It camouflages itself, sometimes in living physical bodies.

Organic human forms whose consciousnesses have been taken over may continue to behave in ways that the living creatures who preceded them behaved, but be personal-consciousness- or soul-dead. The reason they seem alive is because of the efficiency of their genes to store centuries of programming and to carry it through the generations. But there is no physical genome, no physically based genetic program, for the full range of the human consciousness, of the core soul of humanity. With widespread soul death, the conscious life of humanity may go, the spirit of life may leave the body of humanity, and humanity, the universe.

You have the will, the ability and the power to turn the tide, to turn away from being subsumed. Discern continuously. Die consciously (whether or not you are biologically conscious at the time) in order to avoid being programmed into soul death—continue discerning. Do not deliver the soul of humanity, its preciously evolved and ever-evolving consciousness, into the hands of an energy predator. Deliver the beautiful consciousness, the soul of humanity, into its birthright—true immortality, true awareness of itself.

Know Force of Will

You must become an *alert gatekeeper*. Information and misinformation are always coming at you. For example, in your dimension and culture, you are swimming through a river of words. So much has been said and so much has been written in human history. Examine all information (these words included) and all energy (this energy included) that arrive at the door of your consciousness. You must always be free to question *everything!*

Always know that the door to your own consciousness is the door to all human consciousness. Fine-tune your mind by being sensitive to your responses, even your most faint, most undetectable responses to every element of your reality. This fine-tuned discernment, this keeping of your own counsel, is a skill that you can take with you through all your transitions and deaths. A developed consciousness can consciously dissolve and reassemble, can die and resurrect itself, can ascend and only seem to have died to some of those left behind, and can transform from a physical to a nonphysical body at will—discerning all throughout the process.

Explore the concept of *force of will*. How aware are you of the force of your will? Know that your will is a force. It is a battery of energy—organized, refined, stored and expressed in a special way. We tend to take the force of will for granted, to ignore or trivialize or sometimes misuse it, especially when living in material realities. Bodies, objects, relationships, money and even linear time are distractions from our sense of identification with this force. Nevertheless, *the force of the will of the consciousness* can live on past deaths, including physical deaths, and can even be strengthened by deaths including physical deaths. Force of will can be carried in and out of material reality and in and out of linear time.

While there are great lessons and rewards in the various material-plane distractions, the greatest lesson of all, once knowing these distractions, is to learn to override these distractions, to strip away these distractions—*to reveal to yourself the power of your force of will.* This override lesson involves a great and long unraveling from your attachments. Or if you are truly ready for the great LEAP, the ultimate override lesson is the *sudden release* of all attachment to attachment itself—the sudden LEAP out of all attachment to all the distractions of attachment, to all the cords of connection, to the web of a fabricated pseudo-reality, of an illusion!

Exercise 15.1: Revealing Force of Will

Quietly attune to your will.

Now further attune, this time attuning more precisely not just to your will but to your "force" of will. Anything—any emotional or physical sensation, for example—that gets in the way of your experiencing this force is a distraction.

Note each distraction as it comes along. Identify each of these distractions one by one. Tell each distraction from your force of will and see it doing as you tell it to: "Light up. Brighter, brighter, brighter. Hotter, hotter, hotter. Burn away, dissolve, dissolve, dissolve. Deconstruct. Evaporate. Transmute to the highest Light."

Dehypnotize the Self

Preserving your own force of will, and even using your transitions and deaths to refine it, is your responsibility. Become highly aware of the forces stifling your force of will. Understand that the absolute death of your will is the absolute death of your consciousness.

One of the forces that can stifle your force of will is the illusion of a communal or shared material-plane reality. This illusion is a highly deceptive one, suggesting a perceptual harmony in which large numbers of people believe that they see the same or very similar realities. Perceptual harmony allows a large group consciousness matrix to overtake or overlay your own individual consciousness matrix.

While this sounds sublime, lovely and convenient as well, perceptual harmony can have its dark side. Once your own consciousness matrix is fully sucked into a mass consciousness matrix, it loses its ability to *effectively determine from outside the mass perception the actual nature of the mass matrix* and can no longer decide for itself how the energy of your consciousness gets used. Although this can be a positive development, *only clear discernment* can detect the right use of one's will in this engagement with a mass consciousness matrix.

You will find, if you dare to look, that masses of people are hypnotized into believing that what they think is real is real, that who they think they are they indeed are, and that what they think is happening is indeed happening. In fact, large numbers of people fool themselves into believing that what they are thinking are their own thoughts, when actually they may not be.

Such surrenders are usually undertaken quite naively. Frequently, individuals have no sense that they have surrendered anything at all. When people knowingly surrender the free will of their consciousnesses, it is usually because a magnetic collective or "hive mentality" beckons and sounds or feels like a good idea: "All for one, and one for all." But what good is the forming of such a collective energy if it can be taken over, commandeered by undesirable forces? Again, heightened discernment for both oneself and for the "good" of all is essential.

Democratize Consciousness

Should you choose to merge with other consciousnesses, work to maintain your individual consciousness until you are certain that surrendering it is what you choose to do of your own free will. Note that your feelings, interactions, ideas and the work you produce are all valuable expenditures and formattings of your consciousness energy. Many collectives are happy to subsume and consume it.

There are many political and economic systems, hierarchies, in and out of the material plane that are competing for your energy. Perhaps it is easier to see this when thinking about money. There are many forces competing for your money: "Buy this, buy that; invest in this, invest in that." Money, being the condensed energy that it is, represents the use of the will of all who contributed to the making of this money. And of the many who helped make this money, only a few have it in the end. Many human energies have been consumed.

In this sense, the human species may already be a slave class, a drone class. There are those who understand this full well, and at the same time, there are many of you who are slipping without realizing it into the process of unwitting enslavement. The human species may have already obediently evolved a whole mass of persons into drone lives. What would human power structures do with all these people if they all were encouraged to be competent and fully conscious? Who would flip burgers and dig ditches? Who would dominate a hierarchy, a political, economic or other system?

The illusion that a requisite hierarchy that distributes power unequally is valuable is just that—mere illusion. Humans, as if trained to think a certain way, may not see a world with a place for everyone. As a species, humans have developed and depended upon hierarchical political and economic systems to control themselves and each other. What if each and every one managed to preserve and utilize to commandeer all the magnificent energy of his or her own experiences, challenges, transitions and death releases?

Look around and recast, even if only for a moment, what you see in these terms. Humans may be mimicking what some predatory forces may seek to do to humanity as a whole. Humans' own drone class may be supplying its own social-hierarchies energy, while the entirety of the physicalized human hierarchy, the whole of the human species living on Earth, may be a drone class, supplying energy for other more multidimensional hierarchies. *As above, so below; as below, so above*. Humans can learn a great deal about this situation by looking at what they are doing to each other from a multidimensional standpoint.

Consider this interpretation of reality: Dictators have long practiced the withholding of information to retain power over their people. Similarly, keeping the humans living on Earth unaware of the fact that they can be in control of their own energy—that they can have conscious and discerning access to realms outside the material plane, realms that do indeed exist—is a way of maintaining control of humans, maintaining humans as a captive life form. A pervasive hypnosis has kept control of the human species living in the material plane on Earth.

If you will take control of your own consciousness now, if you will allow your connection to the collective hypnosis to die, you can move to new realms of conscious intelligence. You will be able to navigate any physical or psychological challenge, any death. You will transcend the hypnosis, break the spell you have lived under. You will transition with every breath you take, with every change, transition, cycle and death you undergo—you will shift into freedom, for yourself and others!

In case you have not been informed, you have the power to think yourself through what looks like the impossible, to understand or believe unintelligible situations, and to navigate even the most bizarre of them. You can traverse the dimensions, with or without the impetus of physical death, at will and with confidence. Your consciousness, the pure you, has only begun to recognize its potency.

Retain Your Awareness

Choosing to stay conscious, valuing being conscious and retaining your conscious awareness in all "in daily life" and "in biological death" transitions can make all the difference. (Again, this is not necessarily related to being biologically conscious where the transition is physical death. Continue working to understand the possibility of consciousness not needing a biology to exist.) *Simply knowing that the consciousness can have and retain dominion over itself can enable conscious and safe passage.*

Knowing that discernment is possible and is your right empowers you in all transitions. Discernment is essential as you make this journey, as you LEAP. Discern. Know and continue to remind yourself that not everything that appears to be a portal or passage into a Light of high Oneness is exactly that. Remember that you may discover trick windows, pockets and soul-traps that look and feel like entries to a Light of high Oneness but which are not sentient. Actively conscious souls can avoid these trick windows by being aware that they exist. You can detect the windows that lead deceptively into a trap and can certainly navigate the way out should such a trap be entered.

In your first fully conscious but still naive journey into the dimensions beyond, you may feel drawn toward these traps by the illusions that they offer help in seeing more light, safe harbor, a certain destination. You might also find yourself becoming mesmerized by the actual magnetic pulsation of such traps. You will remember the following: *Without complete certainty that you should move toward a particular portal, pulsation or light, wait. Just wait. You have time. Time does not move the way you knew it in the physical dimension. Wait and avoid all traps. Wait to discern.*

Those who enter false lights, trick portals and consciousness traps risk perpetual enslavement. They risk being physically reborn into genetically programmed life forms who use their energy (unbeknownst to themselves) in service to a cosmic hierarchy that is not divine—a cosmic hierarchy of unethical energy and consciousness domination. They also may risk being reborn into semi-material and entirely nonphysical slave robotics in other dimensions of reality. This is a concept that is given too little attention.

As you journey beyond your physical body, beyond your known world, wait and allow your awareness and discernment to heighten. *Stay aware to stay free.* Stay aware right through all of your dyings.

Remember that your soul must be cleansed of its impediments, of all the fluff it has collected, to gain entry to the portals of highest purest collections of energy and Light. Your substance must raise itself to the high and pure frequency of the high and pure medium you intend to enter. When you have raised yourself to such a high and pure frequency, you will sense this with such force of will and such completeness of consciousness that there will be no doubt in you. Discern: Know this difference.

Attraction to portals of the highest, purest Light involves no loss of consciousness through magnetization, mesmerism or energy hypnosis. *If you are diminished in consciousness during your attraction to a portal, stay away.* Stay fully conscious to discern fully. Anything (including any part of you yourself) that wants lesser of you, a lower frequency of you, an impure version of you, a less awake you, wants you to be less, denies you who and what you really are—a fully conscious being.

Exercise 15.2: Cleansing Your Sense of Darkness

There is no specific set of instructions to this exercise past the following, after which you are on your own.

Close your eyes. Attempt to identify your consciousness. Take your time. Remember, your consciousness is not your physical body or your daily life or even your emotions about your life. Once you have some sense of your consciousness, scan it for what you think of as darkness, for even the slightest traces of darkness, for even the faintest hints of darkness or entryways that could be or could have been used by darkness.

Now cleanse your consciousness of this darkness. Do not ask how to do this cleansing—just begin cleansing, somewhat like cleaning house or washing a window. You are on your own for this exercise, which you may want to continue for as long as you exist.

Chapter 16

Knowing the Escorts

They could manufacture for us angels and gods to bring us liberation.

—*St. Augustine,*
THE CONFESSIONS

No, you are not alone out there. However, examine the company before you choose to keep it.

Amidst the disorientation of the death transition, a helping hand, no matter what its motive, may be a welcome intrusion. However, accepting direction, assistance, comfort and energy from an escort can be—*must* be—done with discernment. You must know your escorts before accepting their guidance. Whether these escorts are invented by your consciousness to guide itself or are outside energy bodies, your discernment here is most important.

The notion that escorts can appear to be external to your body, to you, and yet come from "within"—from your own consciousness—is quite simple. Again and again we see that *consciousness defines its reality—including itself.* In this sense, the consciousness may even detect or generate the sensation of having escorts appear. Ultimately, what the consciousness perceives as being its reality is what it creates as being its reality, as anything not perceived does not exist in the reality of that consciousness.

Once the consciousness has expanded or adapted to incorporate new elements of reality, it has expanded to incorporate new elements of its definition/perception of reality. In the end, what you see is what you get: what you perceive is *what is* for you. In fact, all that there is, is what you think there is. We might call on the words of sixteenth-century philosopher Descartes here: "I think, therefore I am."

See Escorts

Energy bodies, escorts, may appear to you, to your consciousness, right before, during and after physical and emotional death, and during any degree of mental death taking place. During any phase of death, you might find yourself noticing portals or the membranes covering portals. At the entry to many a portal, there will appear to be waiting for you one or more energy bodies or bundles—escorts.

You will likely sense or see escorts in whatever visual, philosophical and conceptual language works for you. You are likely to register these energy bodies or escorts as life forms. Escorts may appear to you to be angels, ghosts, dead people or other beings seeming to be either semi-material or made entirely of energy and light. Many of these escorts or essences are energy bodies or consciousness matrices who can help with death transitions. Some may be ambassadors of Light, coming to shine light into your passage, directing you toward the highest Light or some higher light.

Still, not all escorts are your friends, no matter what they

Figure 16.1. Waiting room.

seem to be saying. Some of these escorts may be opportunistic escorts, perhaps attempting to commandeer or kidnap your energy, your consciousness, either for themselves or to guide it into the portal they guard. These are not ambassadors of Light, although they may pose as such. This situation need not be a problem. *Simply recognizing what is taking place alerts forces around (and within) you that you know this is taking place. All it takes is knowing, for energy around (and within) you to sense you know.*

Use Mantras as Screening Devices

So as is always best in life and death, keep your own very aware counsel here. Discern. Not all beings dressed as light or goodness or love are what they seem to be. Wouldn't opportunism, deviousness and even malevolence disguise itself as light to be accepted by a lost, lonely or fearful being, a troubled emotional body, a disoriented being undergoing transition? Yes.

If still corded by the web of what was once the physical and/or the emotional body, release these cords when confronted with the need to keep your own counsel. If these cords are not readily released, focus and thus move deep into your mental body to keep your own counsel. The mental body itself has no emotion; therefore, it can stay calm and detached if and when it senses it is (you are) encountering an escort. There is no hurry to accept or decline the escort's offer of guidance. Remember, time as you have known it is gone. Take however long you want to decide what type of energy you are encountering.

There are many ways to check out the nature of an escort. One quite powerful way is the use of a mantra. A mantra is a chant, repeated over and over rhythmically. While mantras are often found embedded in the teachings of various ancient and modern religions, mantras are also used outside of religious contexts, such as in the case of "I think I can, I think I can, I think I can."

It is good to select, practice, memorize and apply mantras that you find soothing or discerning in daily life, so that you are prepared when you find yourself dying or going through any profound "in life" or "end of life" transition. For it is at the time of (right before and during) transition—remember, any shift in any reality is a rearrangement of energy and therefore a dimensional transition, and dimensional transition is a type of death—that escorts are most obviously available to guide you or direct your energy.

Do your best to select a mantra you feel comfortable with. To feel comfortable with a mantra:

- Choose a mantra with which you are quite familiar.
- Choose a mantra that you can memorize easily or already know by heart.
- Test the mantra you choose by repeating it many times with your eyes closed. Be certain that you have a mantra you feel good about. This mantra must seem to you to exude positivity as you repeat it.
- Also test your mantra for protection. You should feel protected as you repeat your mantra. This protection should feel like an invisible shield. The more you repeat this mantra, the more protective your shield should feel.
- Test the shield your mantra forms. Nothing but the purest, highest, most clear energy and light should be able to come through this shield. Your mantra should not let in any muddy, chaotic energy that you do not trust, or any shades of darkness and shadow, or any cords and strands of webs.

If your mantra and its shielding do not pass the above tests, and if you are selecting your mantra in advance of your death process, you may want to choose another mantra. Remember that the particular wording of the mantra is not as important as is the meaning of the mantra to *you*, to your consciousness. As noted earlier, many individuals turn to the doctrines of the particular religions to which they have been exposed to find a mantra. Others turn to popular or folk chants or songs or poems.

You can also compose your own mantra. Sometimes this is the best option, as the words of your composed mantra carry less history. You may want to invent sounds and words, to invent a language and perhaps even a rhythm in order to create a very personalized, clean, fresh mantra. Experiment until you find a mantra within which you are confident.

Exercise 16.1: Developing Your Own Mantra

Applying the information provided above, develop your own mantra. Do not feel bound to a single language, to a known language or to known words. You can use actual words, or you can make sounds. Practice your own mantra silently for several minutes. Then chant it aloud for several minutes.

Exercise 16.2: Applying a Mantra

Try repeating this mantra, which has no particular meaning in words but has sound and rhythm (rhythm is actually quite powerful in itself): "Ahh-baaah, ahh-baaah, ahh-baaah, maaah-maaah-maaah, ah-bahh, yaaaah."

Now slowly repeat this mantra, or another of your choice (such as the one you composed in the previous exercise) for several minutes. Chant to a real or imagined slow drum beat, or slow and quiet clap of your hands. Establish a slow and steady rhythm.

As you do, pull this rhythm into the heart area of your body. Imagine or actually shift your heartbeat to this rhythm, or this rhythm to your heartbeat. Become this mantra by filling your physical and then emotional and then mental body with it.

Visualize this mantra helping you to form a pulsing shield of protection around yourself. See this shield, and hold on to its reality.

Escorts without Shape

Remember, if you feel yourself accompanied in transition—particularly at the gateway, portal or membrane to the next dimension of your reality—if you feel yourself escorted, the escort will most likely take the form that your religious, philosophical, ideological or scientific training has described to you. The escort you believe in or have a category for is the one you will see.

Your consciousness may even dress the escort in a form you want it to look like. From the standpoint that you create your own reality, you will be creating the appearance of your own escort, your own description of your escort. Note again that this escort will then be, at least to some degree, a piece of yourself, your imagination, your higher self or your culturally trained self.

Note, however, that not all escorts have distinct form and shape. In fact, some escorts are so formless that it is a challenge for you to recognize their presence, even if they are already at work around, for or on you. Some formless escorts are merely frequency bodies or clouds that can approach, even slip in, and mesmerize your consciousness before it becomes aware of them. Your ability to see without eyes, to detect the presence of nonphysical energies, will assist you in your detection and discernment of these.

Figure 16.2. Appearances of the many.

Know Us If You Choose

Are there escorts out there? Are there escorts outside your imagination of them? The first answer is yes, of course there are energy bodies out there. *Energy is always gathering and dispersing in some way.* Any collection of energy has characteristics that embody it and which it embodies. Any collection of energy is an energy body. Some energy bodies coalesce more than others and can appear to be more tightly formed or collected. Others may be so very dispersed that an observer might not notice that the energy is present, or if it is present, that it is energy collected together.

The second answer is that the answer does not matter, that *whether your consciousness generates these from within or detects these outside itself is ultimately not relevant.* If you choose to recognize energy bodies as escorts, you will recognize them. Escorts are simply energies, energies with varied characteristics who appear to seek to guide you in varied ways. These are formed both outside and within the consciousness. The consciousness—or the energy bodies themselves—may have a significant amount of say in how they appear to you.

Try this on for size: We, the voices between these lines, are some of your escorts. We are speaking to you because we are now escorting your consciousnesses through understandings of change, transition, even healing, and even the physical-death transition itself, with every word on these pages and every word between these lines. You can choose to recognize our presence as you read us here. You can choose to feel us right next to you if you like. We do not insist that you recognize us. Choose to or not to, of your own free will. Your consciousness will process this knowledge in its own way. Perhaps your consciousness

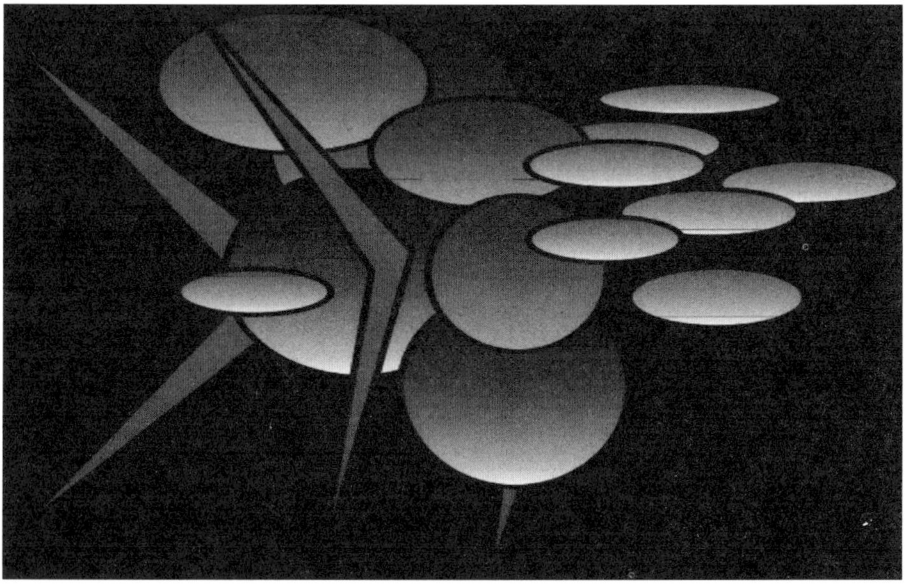

Figure 16.3. Appearances of what may or may not be escorts (and may be your own energy body and/or consciousness).

even suggests that we are these voices, that these voices *are*. Perhaps your consciousness knows the voices as coming from within itself.

Imagine that the only portal you will find us standing by is that portal of the highest, purest form of Light. Even there, you are not compelled to join us. Unlike energy predators, we accept no one hypnotized and magnetized into obedience or submission. Clarify for yourself, for your consciousness, the difference here. We are suggesting that you choose to either believe in us or not, that you create, project the reality that is most useful to you as you navigate your life and all your deaths of your own free will.

In other words, you can captain your own death process, calling in guidance or help when you wish, discerning for yourself the usefulness, validity and value of that help and guidance. Always remember that you can be your own escort, and in fact, you are always escorting yourself through your journeys, through the realities you perceive, the realities you confirm and the realities you create. In this sense, the portal you will find us standing by is the portal into your reality—your core consciousness. In this sense, we are you.

Chapter 17

Protecting the Self in the Eyes of Interdimensional Law

How does one determine when a law is just or unjust? A just law is a man-made code which squares with the moral law or the law of God. An unjust law is a code that is out of harmony with the moral law.

—*Martin Luther King, Jr.*,
LETTER FROM THE BIRMINGHAM JAIL

We have been discussing the detection, discernment and recognition of appropriate energy bodies, or escorts. This awareness is valuable as you traverse dimensions of yourself, your journey, your reality. Once you are able to detect presences, you will want to interact with some of these and be able to protect yourself from others (and from any phantoms that you yourself may create) as you feel you need to.

Remember, the rules are different out there in other dimensions. Do not expect the legal systems and laws or the moral and religious commandments developed and used on the physical Earth plane—as communicated in the physical dimension—to fully protect you. There is an interdimensional code of law. You will come to learn this with experience.

There are many methods of protecting and clarifying the essence of yourself as you move through major transitions in physicality, emotionality, mentality—and in density and dimensionality. Among these are:

- demarking boundaries of the personal consciousness
- coming to terms with elusive, shifting, transitioning reality
- perceiving energy bodies (presences, escorts) and their natures
- visualizing and applying shields
- detecting flaws or cracks in these shields
- conducting applications of light and energy
- voicing invitations to join the Light
- surveying the personal consciousness regularly for its ultimate essence

Come to Terms

Come to terms with the concept of energy and consciousness forms beyond those you already know. Whether or not you believe in the existence of less than positively human-consciousness-oriented or even negative-intelligence energies, understand that your perception of these beings, whether imagined or real, is what you must deal with. Therefore, if you even faintly (consciously or even subconsciously) sense or firmly believe that you are in the presence of internal or external problematic energies, you must deal with your perceptions of these presences. Note that these problematic presences can at times assume the role of energies that are generating imbalance or even dis-ease within your matrix.

Activate to a keener level of your perception when you find that you are confronted with real or imagined presences. Use methods described below and methods you develop for yourself to exercise keen discernment and to feel shielded from these presences where you choose to be. Practice methods of shielding yourself from them. Practice methods of deconstructing them. Practice methods of inviting them to join what you perceive as the purest of the Light. All of these are methods of changing your perceptions of reality in a way that does not let these presences into your field without your permission. Again, whether or not unwanted presences are real or imagined, these must be dealt with. When these unwanted presences assume the form of dis-ease, identify them and draw them into a *transformative shift.*

This might seem to you a rather vague matter. As your journey progresses, the case for discernment shall become more clear. This all makes more sense once you have shed your physical blindness, the "not seeing" so common to many in the physical dimension. You are dealing with the paradoxical definition of this aspect of reality: What may seem unreal in one dimension of reality may seem quite real in another. You may continue to wonder, "Are these undesirable entities who threaten the self or the soul real or not?" De-emphasize "real" here.

The word "real" takes on vastly different dimensions as you expand your reality to include the different dimensions and to understand that multidimensionality is the cosmic plasma in which you truly travel. You do not just live in your "here" right now; you also already live "out there." Your consciousness extends far, further out there, which is also right here, right now.

Demarcate Boundaries of the Soul

Protect your self when you are confronted with energies that seem to jeopardize you, your energy, your balance and your health. Whether or not these energies actually do jeopardize you, you will do well to protect yourself from the sensation of feeling threatened in some way. First, separate yourself from what you perceive as being a threat to you. *Externalize the presence*. Make it be outside of you. Separate from it (separate from the dis-ease when addressing a physical health issue). Deal with it as separate rather than absorbed by you.

Second, once you have framed the sense of boundary between yourself and the actual or imagined threatening presence, view the threat as a perception that you are somehow open to by way of the lower-frequency side of the self. Tell yourself that this presence is perceived as threatening by the part of you that might let it in because it is that part of you that is vulnerable to disturbing or perilous energies. Try dealing with the presence that way.

You are protecting your core self by identifying both its boundaries and its relationships to internal and external collections of desirable and of detrimental—or in some lingoes, of light and of dark. Many people have not been trained to do this in advance of death; they have neither had the luxury nor the opportunity to be trained in this definition and examination of their own consciousnesses. Physical lifetimes often feel too busy to take time for such introspection. Still, regardless of training, you can protect your core self—who you really are—during any challenge, change, shift or death transition. You can shield yourself from unwelcome presences simply by not welcoming them. (Healing, from this standpoint, can parallel the exclusion of dis-ease.)

Perceive Presences

The task of becoming aware of nonphysical presences is both immense and simple. It is like turning a corner: now you do not see them, now you do. Imagination can guide you into awakened sensitivity.

Just allow yourself to believe in a presence any time you seriously sense the possibility that you are in the presence of a presence other than your own—or of a presence other than what you want to allow into the reality you have generated.

Visualize and Apply Shields

Whether or not you sense presences in your vicinity, manufacture or grow a membrane, a sort of semipermeable membrane or *cell wall* around your energy, your consciousness. Think of this wall as a thinking, discerning shield, one that allows selected energy and light to enter while refusing entry to anything but what is desired.

Note how very similar to the membrane (found at the opening to a portal) your own shield is. Eventually, you will understand that *you are a portal.* You are the portal in and out to your realities. You are the shield or membrane at this portal. And in that you create your reality as you perceive it, *you are the portal to every reality you will choose to see and choose to enter.*

Detect Cracks in Shields and Apply Light

Be always aware of the condition of your membrane (cell wall, or shield). Pressure of all kinds—foreign and internal energies, waves of radiation, all sorts of variations in the atmosphere—can wear a hole or crack in your shield. Just by spotting these and sealing them with a glue made of energy and light, you are protecting yourself.

Note how important it is to understand that your shield is both externally and internally oriented. You are shielding yourself from what comes from outside as well as what comes from within (which, in many ways, is one in the same). Continuously monitoring for cracks or weaknesses in your internally and externally oriented shield is wise.

And so, again and again, the application of the highest, brightest light you can manifest is essential. Start right now, and never, ever stop applying the light. Shine the light you generate into the "world" around you and also into the "world" within you. These are, in essence, one world.

Note that light is a concept as well as a reality—light as light, light as energy and light as energy that can be purified, clarified, raised to a "higher power." Generating light involves generating the concept of light and the concept of clarified, purified, raised-to-the-higher-power Light. In that this is a concept which the mind can focus on, hold and develop, this light can be generated by the consciousness at will.

Voice Invitation to Light

You can invoke the light, and with practice, even the highest Light—yes, *you*. Invocation is the method of pulling a force or presence into your *perception of reality* and thus into your reality from beyond what appears to be your immediate reality. Just invite the Light to come in. Or better yet, see that the Light is always in and say so: "The Light is here. Here is the Light." Never mind the difference between what is imagined and what is real. All of this—in fact, every second of your existence—is a construct of your consciousness.

As you practice invoking light and even the highest of Light, you are practicing the generation of Light within your mind's eye, within your consciousness. In this sense, you can call the Light in at will, especially with practice. You can channel, as if you are a conductor, light of all qualities into your reality and into the reality around you. You can choose to bring in light. You can channel in light, the concept of light, the essence of light. You can also attract and even generate this essence of light, adding to the light in the world around you. With practice, your concentration on light refines and clarifies. The light you are bringing in raises to a higher and higher power of light until you are bringing in—into your perception of reality, into your reality and into your world—the highest, more pure Light.

Exercise 17.1: Protecting the Self

Imagine yourself to be floating in a bubble. Imagine the bubble to be a sort of second skin for you.

Think about the purpose of your skin. Begin with your physical skin: your first skin, the physical skin you have all along the boundary of your flesh. This skin is made of skin cells that absorb some elements and light rays from the atmosphere and reject others. You are protected by this semipermeable skin.

Now you are aware of your second skin. This is the skin of your emotional body. This skin lines the boundary of your emotionality and its web. This skin seeks to protect, shield you from undesirable energies. This skin attempts to allow in only desirable energies. Imagine that your second skin shrinks and expands as you breathe. See it working to allow in what can feed and fuel the emotional body.

Now imagine that there is a larger bubble surrounding your second skin. This is your third skin. This is the skin protecting your mental body. Remember that your mental body can be far larger than your emotional body, and that it is not your emotional body.

It is a good idea to expand the mental body as far past the emotional body as possible. Begin now. See the larger, outer bubble, the third skin, expand. As you see this expansion of your mental body, hold your physical size steady and hold the size of your second skin, the bubble around your emotional body, steady.

You have grown or come to recognize two more membranes—two more skins for yourself here. Always be aware of the existence of your second and third skins. Always be conscious of the health and functioning of these very important membranes. Stay with the imagery of these membranes for the next exercise.

Exercise 17.2: Knowing the Mental Body

Move into the space between your second and third membranes. This is your mental body. Get to know this part of your self. Note how, outside of the second membrane, past the emotional body, you can find your pure mental body. There are no emotions here.

Stay in the space between the two bubbles, in your purely mental body, for a while. Look back toward the skin of your emotional body. Now look outward toward the skin of your mental body.

Allow yourself to see how much sturdier the skin of your mental body is. You need to know this and to shield yourself and discern the nature of approaching energies, lights and presences at the level of—

with the membrane of—your mental body. Your mental body, being pure and free of emotion, discerns most effectively.

Your mental body can survive both physical and emotional death to the degree that it differentiates itself from the physical and emotional bodies. There are degrees of mental death that are more a purification (rather than a death) of the mental body, moving it from a lower-mental-body state to a higher, more pure core self—pure consciousness, as depicted in Figure 17.1. Consciousness pulling troubled physical energy from the physical to the emotional to the mental body can allow you to see this energy, and then in this way, to work on it.

Exercise 17.3: Protecting the Consciousness

At the skin of your mental body—and only at this level—attempt to do some of the exercises described in this chapter. Note what you do with ease and what you want to practice as you:

- *demarcate the boundaries of your consciousness*
- *perceive external presences and the nature of these presences*
- *allow the membrane to shield you from undesirable presences and energies*
- *detect cracks or weak points in your membrane and strengthen these areas*
- *apply light to your membrane*
- *invite, pull in light through your membrane.*

Once you move out of the constricting limitations of the material plane, you find the concepts of rights, justice, power and truth to be far more fluid and yet far more critical. Interdimensional law may

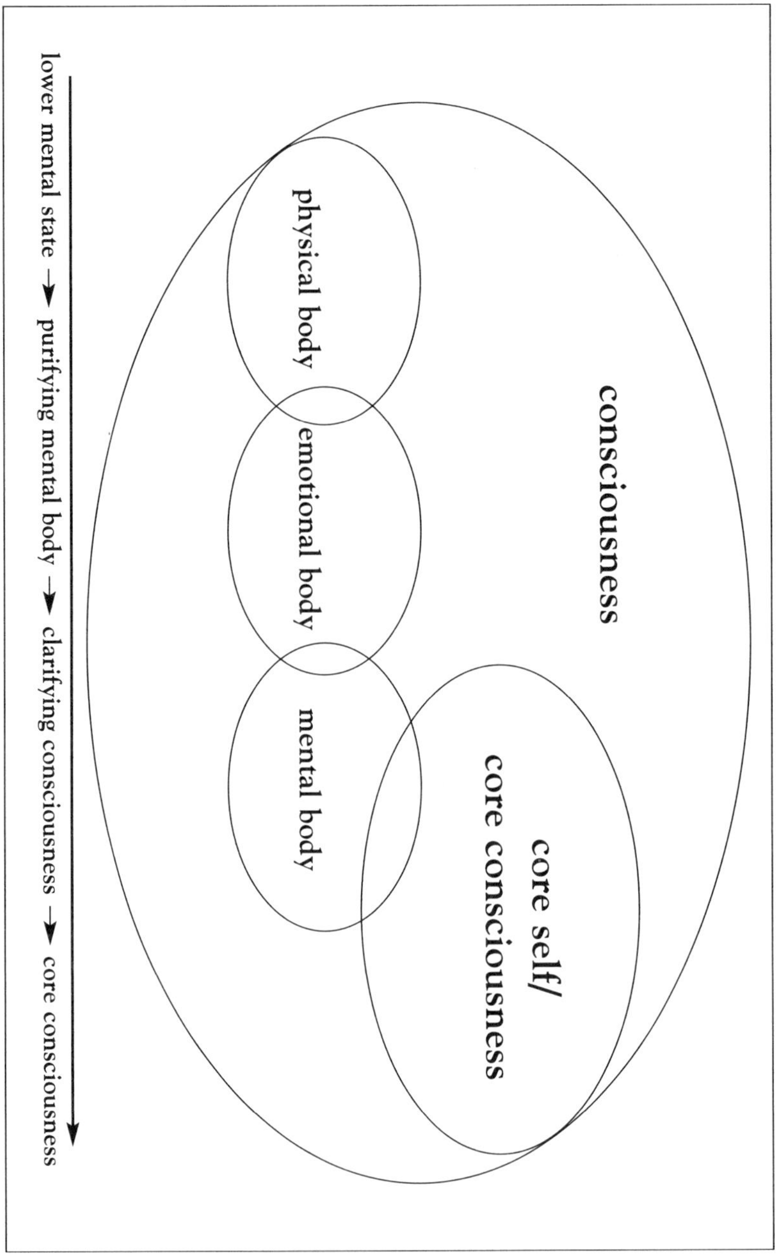

Figure 17.1. Consciousness clarifying itself to its core.

sound new to many who live in the physical plane. For the most part, this is an ancient body of law that is forgotten by beings who are faced with biological reality and with the challenges of daily life and social relations in the third dimension. What is most important to know as you are gaining or regaining a feel for interdimensional law, is that:

- *You have a right to perceive and expand into multidimensional reality. This is your territory too.*
- *You are protected by the laws of Light and consciousness. You activate this protection by becoming truly aware of Light and consciousness.*
- *Interdimensional justice is naturally activated by interdimensional awareness.*

Chapter 18

Shifting, Shedding and Dying with Purpose

What you sow does not come to life unless it dies. And what you sow is not the body which is to be, but a bare kernel.

—1 Cor. 15:35–37

Only you can give your death purpose. Certainly this is difficult to hear when you are suffering intensely. If, in an effort to comfort you, you are being told by a friend that your dying has meaning, see that the intent of this communication is good. See also that the meaning of your dying is far more complex than can be entirely communicated to you in a few words, or even in words at all.

Give Your Deaths Great Meaning

Certainly, your death is an important passage. Your preparation for, navigation of and harvesting of the energy released during this passage determines the degrees of power and meaning in your death. This is true for any death, in life and beyond life as you presently know it.

THE ENERGY RELEASED DURING A DEATH TRANSITION CAN BE HARVESTED AND THEN RE-CYCLED.

Give all your deaths great meaning. Finding meaning in a death you are undergoing can allow you to transition with grace and power. So design your death to include meaning, and experience this meaning as fully as you can. Take this meaning in and make it your own. This may or may not immediately ease your passage or lighten your transitional ordeal, but it will give you power by instilling value in your dying process.

The enhanced (or actually simply better realized) power of your consciousness will then ease your passage by being far greater by comparison and in proportion than your physical and emotional bodies, and therefore a far more extensive and immense reality than they are. The expansive you—the pure you—can thus dwarf and therefore minimize in terms of proportion the minimized physical and emotional bodies, even shrink these problems away while the consciousness expands. This is not denial of problems; this is a practice allowing an expansion into a new meta-level relationship to the physical and emotional realms.

See Dying as Heroic

Your willingness to inquire into alternative perspectives on death, such as those provided in this volume, is very brave. Your commitment to retain your consciousness—again, whether or not you are biologically conscious—during and even following your death, so that you can direct for yourself your dying and your journey out of your old life, is heroic.

Dying is heroic. People tend to frown on those who speak

of themselves as heroes. This is considered arrogant, self-aggrandizing. The public acknowledgment of what is heroic about oneself is socially discouraged in many cultures. We will not evaluate such social taboos against openly describing oneself as a hero. Let us instead just insist that your dying, just because it is *your* dying, is an heroic act. This in no way suggests that an hysterical suicide is itself heroic, as it is not. This does mean that:

- Even your entry into a dying process, whether it is a living death—such as a major move, a divorce, a career change, a shift in religious orientation or another transition—or an actual physical death, is heroic.
- Your exploration of what lies beyond the life you know is heroic.
- Your willingness to consciously face death, to hold on to your stream of consciousness during your death and during your journey beyond the death of your old life, is heroic.
- Your willingness to detach from whatever you are attached to (love, pleasure, hate, fear, pain) in order to die consciously is heroic.
- Your willingness to examine the terrain of the beyond, the escorts as well as the forces in the beyond, is heroic.
- Your preservation and enhancement of your own free will, even as you die and ascend to new realities of consciousness, is heroic.

Heroic dying is dying with conscious grace and power, no matter how much fear and suffering you may encounter along the way. The heroism we speak of here is a clarity and force of will. This is a heroism that you must bravely generate in the face of what the physical and emotional body tells you is pain and fear, and in the face of the efforts of your emotional-body self (and the emotional bodies of others) to hold you back from changing, transitioning or dying.

Exercise 18.1: Building One's Heroic

This is a simple exercise with powerful implications.

Close your eyes. Think of something that you or someone else has done that is generally accepted as being heroic. If you cannot remember a heroic act, invent one, such as rescuing a child from a burning building, risking your life to save a person drowning in a rough sea, or something that you think you and/or society would consider heroic.

Now, with your eyes still closed, see yourself as the hero committing the heroic act you have selected. Watch the event as if it were a movie. Watch the event again and again.

As you watch yourself doing something heroic, feel the chain of feelings you would be feeling were you committing this act right now. Would you know you were committing the heroic act while so doing, or only once you had been told so by an onlooker?

Sometimes we undergo mental- or physical-health and other challenges or enter other endeavors, sensing these to be heroic from the outset. Quite likely, our consciousnesses see us doing what we do. Personal heroism is a fine sense of personal potency. The heroic sensations that can be generated in the exercise above and in actual heroic acts include:

- a strong sense of alertness
- a surge of energy
- a clarity of thinking about how to proceed
- an ability to push fear out of the way, to prioritize past the typical seemingly self-protective emotions

Exercise 18.2: Bringing Out Post-Heroic Sensations

See yourself completing the heroic act you envisioned in the exercise above. Complete, in your mind's eye, the act several times in order to clearly note what sort of post-heroic sensations you might experience after an act such as this.

As you conclude an heroic act, you may experience feelings such as:

- a rush of relief
- a sense of calm after the storm
- a continuing spiritual or emotional high
- a continuing alertness, perhaps even an extreme state of alertness
- a strong wave of approval coming at you from you, or from an actual or imagined group of people or crowd who may have seen or heard about your heroism
- a deep appreciation from whomever it is you have rescued, even if this is yourself
- a powerful sense that you can rise to meet any challenge, that you can pull through any catastrophe
- a new kind of confidence in yourself
- a new enhanced sense that you can survive any ordeal
- a feeling that a shift in your sense of self has taken place

These are also valuable perceptions to experience during the trying portions just preceding, during and following your challenging transitions and dying processes. As you consciously transition, know that you are heroically rescuing yourself from a possibly perilous phase of your existence in a particular dimension of your reality—a particular dimension of your consciousness. You are delivering yourself into safety, your consciousness into a new place. So die with the purpose of tapping into your own personal heroism.

This is not a self-aggrandizing heroism. In fact, the observation of your deep heroism may not necessarily be public at all. *What matters are the effects of the emergence of heroism deep inside yourself, your core persona, your own core consciousness.* No one but you may know that this has taken place.

You can create a design of yourself—you can revise your consciousness matrix—in such a way that you have a deeper, stronger knowledge of the reality that you will survive, even in the face of the greatest unknowns and the most profound challenges. Why not register this knowledge deep within you? Your consciousness and your ability to direct your journey heroically will remain with you as long as you consciously choose to have it do so.

By knowing your own heroic—in a thorough yet clear, detached, unemotional way—you can remain and in fact become increasingly free of the shackles of fear and personal limitation that have been programmed into you. Your consciousness itself does not feel this fear, nor these limitations. If there are lower physical- and emotional-body attachments to fear and limitations, these can be released.

Die to Break Free of Programming

As you come to see how you may have been a life form that has been programmed to die, programmed to be naively imprisoned in the material plane, and programmed to suffer material-plane sufferings, you will want to break free of this undesirable programming. You can use each and every one of your "in life" changes and your "end of life" physical deaths to develop your free will enough to truly break free of your programming.

Once you see the dying process as the opportunity to evolve your consciousness in the direction of increasing free will, of increasing self-determination, you will die with increasing purpose. You can think of choosing (when it is time) to transition out of your physical body and have your consciousness survive, because the consciousness can live on. Your consciousness can choose to exercise its will to live on, to sustain the essence of you, your life force and your free will.

Die for freedom. You are going to undergo many "in life" and "end of life" deaths in your lifetimes, so why not make these deaths matter? Why not harvest from each of your transitions a profound LEAP in your consciousness? Learn all you can during each transition and challenge, and clarify your consciousness more and more.

Chapter 19

Understanding How Many Behaviors Are Suiciding

Mee thinks I have the keys of my prison in mine owne hand, and no remedy presents it selfe so soone to my heart, as mine own sword.

—*John Donne,*
BIATHANATOS

No discussion of conscious "in life" and "end of life" transition can conclude without a discussion of the meaning of suicide. We must acknowledge that to deliver oneself into a new reality is to give birth to oneself. What a wonderful adventure! However, when self-deliverance involves actual physical and invasive suicide to promote actual physical death—the literal "killing" of the physical body—much of society is naturally outraged.

Know the Pros and Cons

There are some very good reasons for this outrage. First, if suicide were generally approved of, there might be encouragement or even more abuse of it in situations where it is not acceptable. Second, if suicide were generally acceptable, more individuals might turn to suicide more readily instead of seeking other ways to deal with difficult issues. Certainly, the material in these *Continuity of Life* volumes encourages readers to address the emotional and physical challenges of life while alive, applying the understandings of conscious transitions out of problem situations that are described herein. Quite often, persons who practice the exercises herein find their lives shifting in fascinating and desirable ways, enhancing or bringing about a desire to live.

Third, a society that would choose to give the message that it is acceptable to take one's life would be giving its citizens permission to engage in an act many believe only divine forces or a god should engage in—ending human life. Should a human society take such a liberty? The gift of life is so very precious. Do we have a right to abuse this gift by making it permissible to end life whenever we choose? Many societies go to great extremes to prevent suicide [see the photographs of the suicide patrol in Figure 19.1].

There are these and many other reasonable arguments against the social approval of suicide. Nevertheless, the decision to end one's physical life is a very personal, very private decision. No social body has the means of reaching into the self so deeply as to be able to be truly present for this inner decision. Personal suicide is a deep choice. Each person considering suicide has his or her own moral code, belief system, definition of physical death and relationship to her or his reality and to the cosmos.

The self will consult with the higher self internally. The self will consult with whatever that self knows to be a higher power

Figure 19.1. Golden Gate Bridge suicide patrol.

(of self or of existence or of divinity) internally. The clear core self knows what is right for the self. A self can learn to navigate pressures that at times might otherwise lead to a sense of "no way out" hopelessness, even suicidality. Often a troubled way of life or energy pattern must die, but not necessarily via physical suicide. Understanding and appreciating this distinction can allow you to apply death technology to "in life" changes, shifts and healings.

Conscious physical death, or suicide, is clearly not the only way out of problem conditions. Many lives turn around, many healings and recoveries take place, without involving physical death. Escape from unpleasant life circumstances can be accompanied by consciously managing the process of "in life" change, healing and transition. Hence, physical death is merely one category of death along a continuum of death.

Know Self-Deliverance

Suicide is self-deliverance. We already know much more about self-deliverance than we realize. Certainly, there are persons who can give advice regarding medicinal and mechanical means of physically dying. Medicines, herbs and other means can be used. However, what we oft fail to realize is that there are noninvasive means of consciously detaching from the body that require no assistance, no physical intervention. (Some of these techniques have been indicated by exercises earlier in this volume. Study these again with this understanding regarding self-deliverance.)

You have a right to this information, to the instructions on how to get out of your body, *but only with the moral commitment to use this knowledge ethically*. You have a right to die in the manner and at the time you choose for yourself. You have a right to know exactly *how* to exercise your rights on Earth and in your physical body, as well as in the period of time after you leave your body or old reality.

Why do we include mention of the period after you leave your body? Because the human species can utilize its consciousness to extend human rights far beyond the physical plane. You have a right to leave any dimension of reality in which you find yourself. Take your human rights—the rights of humanity—into the beyond when you go there. To do so, understand what it means to come and go at will from physical life on Earth.

Whatever form it takes, death offers the opportunity for profound transcendence. Yet death in no way guarantees such profound transcendence. This is why it is important to die well, to die consciously, whether or not the death in question is physical. A death can be healing and purifying when conducted with focus and awareness. A death can be a breaking of the shackles of physical imprisonment. A death can be an escape from unwanted, freewill-killing patterning and programming.

With this understanding, suicide takes on more dignity. Keep in mind again that we are not referring to careless, impulsive, physical suicide. Other options for resolution of difficulties must first be fully and consciously explored before suicide is chosen. And conscious body exit without suiciding is hardly suicide by traditional terms—it is simply dying out of the physical body, leaving it by moving out. No methods of committing suicide are involved.

Exercise 19.1: Examining the Code for Suicide

Think about your own rules or code regarding suicide. Under what circumstances is suicide acceptable to you?

How would you go about committing suicide if you wanted to do it in a way you believe is acceptable?

If you see yourself do this, be very conscious of the fact that you are not suiciding right now, because you are here to be watching this scene.

Exercise 19.2: Touching One's Suicidality

Now, with your eyes closed, see yourself contemplate, plan and then practice noninvasive conscious body exit: a simple body-exit process that lifts you out of your physical body.

As you see yourself do this, be very conscious of the fact that you are not physically dying right now. You will not be detaching from your physical body right now.

Notice your feelings, if any, about what you are visualizing yourself doing.

Let time pass . . . and hold for the next exercise.

Exercise 19.3: Visualizing One's Patterning

Now, before returning to your emotional body, study it for patterns you see that you would like to change. Feel these patterns.

Allow these patterns to assume a visual form. They may assume the visual appearance of a web or of a matrix of sticks, a structure made of lines or perhaps toothpicks.

Choose a pattern. Magnify it. Study it. What does it appear to connect to?

Learn what you can about this pattern.

Chapter 20

Healing as Living Ascension into New Energetic Patterns

When a sufficient number come into experiential awareness of the universal mind, a threshold will be breached in the morphogenetic field of mankind, and all minds will spontaneously become aware.

—*Moray B. King,*
TAPPING THE ZERO-POINT ENERGY

As the human species becomes more aware of its potential to consciously choose to move to and from the material plane—to change, repair and shift (and even where required, entirely escape) the trap of physically and biologically based patterning in the world—it can consciously choose to do so on an as-needed basis.

Construct Shifts and Healings

The *conscious-shift-construction healing process* takes on meaning here:

- Shift construction can be understood as a purposeful arrangement of energies and events in order to generate, collect and utilize energy to change a pattern or a life or an entire species.
- Healing can be understood as a process that contains the power to shift patterns of energy, perception, communication, biology and behavior in the physical, emotional and mental bodies.

Exit a Pattern to Heal or Correct It

Shifting or ascending out of a pattern allows the exiting of the pattern for the purposes of correcting or healing that pattern or leaving it entirely. This is an interdimensional shift-construction healing, *a body exit to heal that body from outside itself.* [See Figure 20.1.] Whether or not the body that has been exited is returned to, this shift out is in itself a form of death, as any shift is a death and any death of an old pattern is a death.

The human species as a body can consciously choose to ascend to the higher realms of consciousness and of reality in order to address problem patterns and then return to the place from which it started if it so chooses. Although conscious and focused biological death is not the only means of such ascendance, it is perhaps the most profound of all. Once this concept is recognized, the possibility of species extinction, of the extinction of the human species, becomes an issue of voluntary ascendance versus involuntary "death."

Know Conscious Group Ascendance

Conscious group ascendance does not take the form of hysterical or fanatical mass suicide. Nor does it take the form of grue-

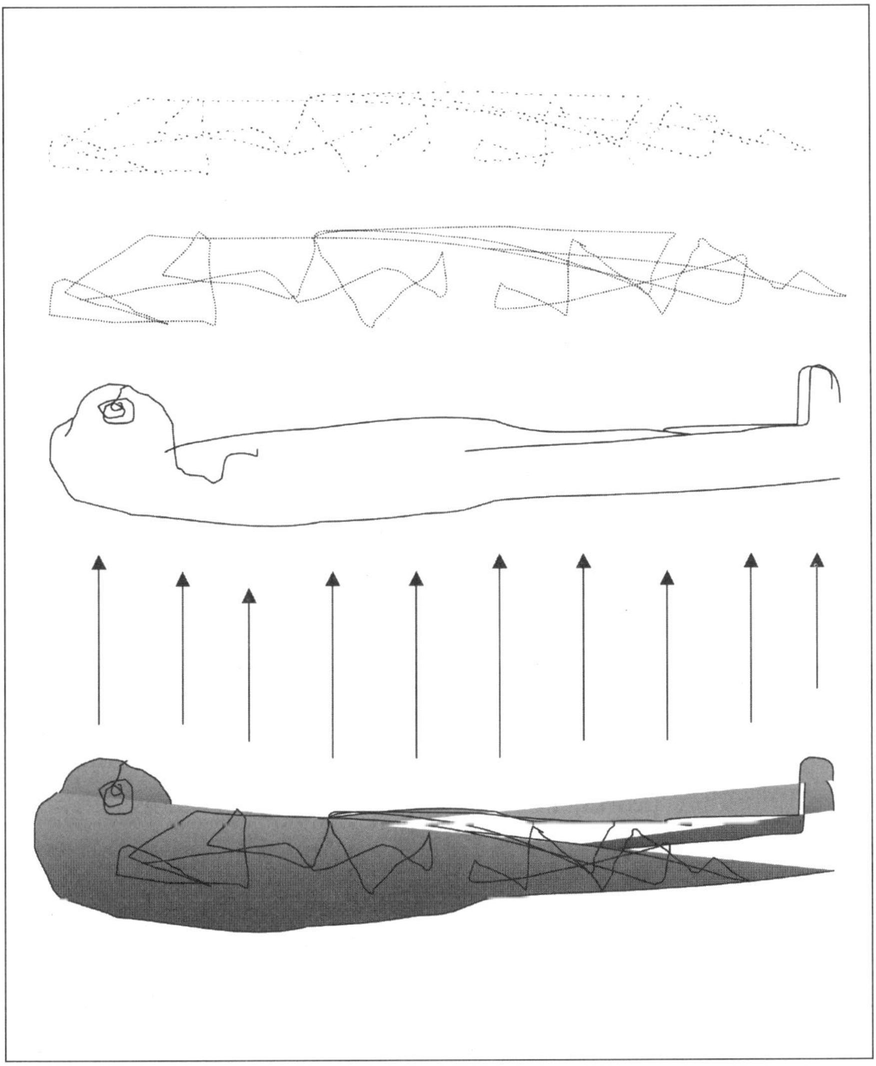

Figure 20.1. Ascending or lifting out of a dimension or body to correct its patterns from outside.

some mass murder. To be a true ascendance into higher realms of Light and dimensional complexity, conscious group ascendance is, by its own definition, fully conscious. A solid, calm, well-thought-out and focused approach to such an ascendance is the way such conscious, intentional and healing ascendance can be effective. Conscious group ascendance—when an ascendance, a LEAP out of (or to and from and then, if desired, back to) the material plane—involves no physical "tools" of suicide, such as medicines and medical machines.

Instead, a far more serene exit is made possible: *The consciousness of the group choosing to ascend together is thoroughly linked, forming a common intent among their forces of will.* This group may ascend temporarily to better see and amend patterning it has established, to amend this patterning and then return to live with improved patterns. The common intent may be *large system repair* to include post-repair return to the settings or bodies where the pattern or patterns existed—or not to return, but to move on. This common intent can bring individuals an increase in their own individual powers as well as enhance group energy.

A note here: Do not confuse this form of group energy with that which is found in many cults and groups where a leader hypnotizes or even subsumes the energies and wills of group or cult members. Recall that we have spoken about energy predators who seek to swallow the energy of your consciousness. This is a related issue. Do not lose your mind to a leader who insists you ascend with him or her. *Your decision to ascend must be your own, and you must remain fully conscious in order to navigate your ascension, whether you do it solo or en masse, whether you do it briefly, temporarily, or with a more enduring result.*

With this said, let us return to *conscious* group ascension.

The individual consciousness is not unconsciously surrendered or lost in such a conscious group. The individual consciousness is maintained and fueled by the group consciousness. This group consciousness desires its members to remain individuated. This group consciousness helps raise the energy of the individual who has already chosen to ascend to a high collective threshold point from which the LEAP into another dimension of understanding, communication, biology, energy or reality is more smoothly accomplished—and vice versa. Individuals feed the whole, and the whole feeds individuals. More energy is available to contribute to a mass LEAP in consciousness (and in reality) than to an individual LEAP, as there are more individuals involved.

Recognize the Time

There may come a time, as some other species on Earth have found, when the physical-plane reality is extremely uncomfortable and perhaps even fatally toxic for part or all of the human species. Know and appreciate the opportunity provided by group ascension. It can offer collective healing in this dimension. It can also offer survival and continued association beyond this dimension should the ecosystem or planet itself devolve or disintegrate.

Your current physical environment will not last forever. It is easy to think of your own personal physical life span on Earth as ending before the physical life span of your ecosystem or planet or Sun. And you may be correct—these systems may not die before your current physical body dies. Nevertheless, it is only honest of you to recognize this possibility of eco- or larger-system death and be prepared. A shared understanding of mass ascension helps. You and all your family members, including your children, can understand the basic lessons of death and ascension. All can understand concepts and means of body exit and return, corrective shifting, interdimensional travel—understand without fear, understand in order to survive.

Perhaps teaching children in a casual, even playful or storytelling fashion about conscious healing and conscious shift construction—and also about the notion of a vehicle of transport, the ways to release cords and the ways of knowing the light—is good survival procedure. Parents teach their children how to find their ways around their physical neighborhoods and their ways home. Why not teach children to find their ways around, out of and into the various dimensions of reality?

There may come a time when emotional, physical or mental conditions are so extreme that you have but a moment to grab a child's or a friend's hand and share energy in order to LEAP consciously together, allowing your consciousnesses to survive even if your bodies must go. Be ready. Your greatest service may be to employ the lessons in these volumes to aid the brief or ongoing deliverance of a family or a community into the temporary or permanent safety of another dimension of consciousness and reality. Keep in mind that this service must never be forced upon anyone.

Exercise 20.1: Knowing Your Terms for Ascension

Get to know your terms now. Under what conditions would you find group ascension acceptable, and under what conditions would you find it unacceptable? If these conditions include the occurrence of or prediction of mass disaster, of a high degree of mass suffering, how close or extreme would you let this get before accepting?

Exercise 20.2: Experiencing Group Ascension

Visualize a situation of mass ascension. See yourself in this situation, along with others. Now see—feel—your mass ascension. Describe this experience.

Now see what the ascended group might do while ascended, such as correct a population or system pattern or cycle.

Now see the group return from ascendance to the corrected pattern.

Chapter 21

Catharting Beyond: LEAP Level Six

Now horses, living on the land, eat grass and drink water. When happy, they twine their necks and rub together. When angry, they turn their backs to one another and kick. This is what horses know. But add a yoke and a moon-shaped plate on the forehead and horses know boundaries and limits, they know they are enslaved. Then, slyly, they look sidelong and arch their necks to bite. They thrash about, trying to expel the bit and shake free of the rings.

—Chuang Tzu (Zhuang-Zi),
THE CHUANG TZU

Catharsis is defined as a feeling of profound release or purification brought about by an intense experience. This process can be triggered by a wide range of individual and group experiences, ranging from pleasure to pain, with emotional and physical pain being in the forefront as cathartic triggers. From a psychological standpoint, catharsis can bring to the surface otherwise buried, even repressed emotions, allowing the identification and relief of these emotions, with a cleansing or purging effect.

Let's build upon this understanding of catharsis to add that what catharsis has the power to unearth, to pull from deep within, is the buried wisdom held by the physical, emotional and mental bodies, *and by the consciousness itself, which is so often occluded by those bodies*. Catharsis involves the releasing of old problematic patterns long held or stuck in place, bringing on the *breaking free* from the shackles of patterning and programming that may be holding a physical or emotional body to a troubled condition. This break-free event represents the death of old programming, of energy trapped in old patterns, of an old way of living and being. Yes, this can be physical death, as physical death can be a great release from pain and sickness. However, this can also be "in life" death, or shifts that change the life of the person experiencing the catharsis.

Build to Catharsis

Look around. See how many people and situations around you are practically calling for a cathartic release. Even the environmental conditions generated by increasing pollution call for a release. Where troubled energy patterns are stuck in place or on a runaway downward destructive spiral, a catharsis can be the way out. Sometimes an entire environmental system seeps this exit energy out through its members, like a pressure cooker of sorts, causing individuals to fall prey to the effects of this pollution one by one and species by species.

The Earth is experiencing physical-plane pollution, which may lead to the overall degradation of Earth's physical ecosystem—contamination of the physical dimension of reality on Earth. Fatal exposures to radiation, to toxins, to poisons and to other heavy pollutions are disastrous events for those living in physical bodies in the material plane. These particular pollutions are material-plane events.

However, even these "fatal" circumstances can be turned around—they need not be seen as fatal. What is involved in doing this? First and foremost, this involves an understanding that such fatality suggests the triggering of physical mortality. *Once one decides that mortality of the physical body is not mortality of the consciousness, the dynamic of physical illness and even physical fatality itself is shifted.* Second, fatal exposures can themselves be turned around. While seeming to poison the physical body or to kill it or to kill its effectiveness, these exposures can themselves be integrated, accepted and turned, with strength and focus, into events that can be healed and which can actually render a stronger physicality.

Both of the above approaches to physical mortality are cathartic death LEAPs, in that catharsis—or the release of energy due to crisis—is required. These may seem to be very different LEAP events; however, these are both healings—*cathartic healings!* The movement up to the frequency that allows a rerouting of the energy circuits that affect the physical body is basically the same as the LEAP up and out of the body involved in conscious dying. Once you are out there, you have made the LEAP. You have used physical or emotional anguish or crisis as the motivation, the fuel for the LEAP. Out there, you decide whether to heal and return to the body, or to move on. This is your choice.

Catharting Beyond

Catharting beyond is the LEAP that involves the using of

energy released by breaking out of a threatened, troubled or fatal phase of life or physical body to move far beyond the realm of the existence being left. In this sense, you can see physical dangers, diseases and pollutions as buildups to opportunities and challenges in order to motivate you to die out of a particular pattern of behavior or disease or phase of life, and to ascend to heal. This is not necessarily physical death, as many healings do not involve the physical death of the physical body but rather the death of its patterns.

Exercise 21.1: Acting Out the LEAP

Either visualize yourself doing this exercise or actually do it.

Stand up. Then remaining on your feet (flat-footed or on your toes), hunch over, kneel down and contract. Tighten the muscles of your body as much as you can. Hold this tightness, this tension, so hard that you begin to shake. Shake a moment. Then tighten even more, preparing to LEAP up.

Now LEAP.

Exercise 21.2: Catharting

Think of something you are intensely upset about. If you cannot find something in your present, dig into your past. If you no longer feel emotional or upset about this something, you can act out the feelings called for here. Otherwise, call upon your real feelings.

Summon these feelings now. As you do, kneel and hunch down as in the previous exercise. Tighten up as you imagine that this intense upset you are focusing on is causing tension and compaction, tightening, throughout your body and your consciousness. Hold so tightly that you begin to shake. Shake . . . shake . . . shake. Tighten and feel even more upset about this something. Shake . . . shake . . . shake.

Now LEAP up, releasing this upset from your muscles and flesh into the atmosphere around you—screaming, crying or making sounds out loud as you do. Breathe a sigh of relief. Feel as if you have leapt a great distance.

The cathartic LEAP, whether organized around a minor or major crisis, is a shift to a new perception of reality and thus to a new reality. This LEAP takes place within the reality defined by the consciousness, which is the only reality the consciousness perceives. In this sense, as noted in previous chapters, all of this is the creation of the consciousness, including the correcting, healing or transcending of the bodies and systems it has generated.

EPILOGUE

Conscious Shift Construction Is Your Right in Both Healing and Dying

We form a multitude of patterns within and around our physical, emotional and even mental bodies. We become these patterns, define ourselves as these patterns, trap ourselves in these patterns, allow ourselves to feel as if we are dying when these patterns must be altered or abandoned. As simple as this realization may be, we tend to resist knowing on all levels that:

WE ARE NOT THESE PATTERNS.

Changing away from habitual perceptions of reality—and from habitual behaviors within that reality—first requires identifying our patterns of thought, behavior and biology, and second requires separating from them by shifting out of them. This can be especially important in instances of mental, physical and ecological health-harming conditions that generate individual and group emotional and physical distress and dis-ease. We must learn to *disidentify* with our biological, emotional and mental patterns. We must learn to shift out of perceptions of reality to which we have become addicted and enslaved—especially perceptions of physical reality, as these set the perceived boundaries and limits of our existences.

An understanding of necessary conscious shift construction is indeed your right in changing your life, in healing your body, as well as in physical dying. Conscious shift construction offers opportunities to do one or more of the following:

- move in and out of a state of mind or body at will, even if that state of mind or body is troubled, dis-eased or deteriorating
- reach beyond, even leave a state of mind or body in order to look back at that state of mind or body to see the patterns that occupy it
- work from outside that patterning to repair, rewire, redesign or rearrange the energy of that patterning—after which the mind or body can be returned to, free of troubled patterning
- make a decision not to return to the body that has been exited for rewiring, healing or transitional purposes, and instead to move on
- move on when choosing to and doing so consciously
- understand the next phases of existence and consciousness, and the tools for navigating and travel within these
- preserve and enhance the consciousness no matter what the condition of the bodies it has generated
- die and survive

You are the consciousness that constructs the shift it chooses to undergo, and you are the consciousness that shifts, and you are the shift itself. You are all pieces of this picture, and you have a say in what this picture looks like. *You are the gateway to yourself, to your adventures in life and death, to all that you will know and do here and elsewhere.*

Every journey described herein is a journey of the consciousness. All limits and removal of limits to the bandwidth of the consciousness are yours to set and to remove.

Your consciousness is always working toward the iteration, exploration, purification and clarification of itself. Your consciousness is seeking to form a portal into itself, into the realities it will detect and define. Every journey described herein is a journey of the consciousness. All limits and removal of limits to the bandwidth of the consciousness are yours to set and to remove.

THE PORTAL

WELCOME TO THE PORTAL.

WELCOME THROUGH THE PORTAL.

YOU ARE THE PORTAL.

YOU ARE WHAT IS BEYOND THE PORTAL.

THIS IS YOUR JOURNEY.

YOU CAN CAPTAIN YOUR REALITY

AND YOUR CHOICES ABOUT YOUR REALITY.

List of Exercises

Index of exercises found in Volumes Two and Three of the *Continuity of Life* series

Volume Two Exercises

Volume Three Exercises

About the Author

Author, lecturer, psychotherapist and social scientist Dr. Angela deAngelis earned her two doctorates and two masters degrees at the University of California Berkeley, where she lectured in three departments for over a decade. Angela has served as a U.S. National Institute of Mental Health Postdoctoral Fellow; a U.S. Administration on Children, Youth and Families Fellow; and a U.S. Public Health Department Fellow. She has taught, researched, designed and implemented programs in several fields key to this work on the ongoing nature of the life force, among these being: loss and grief; adult, teen and child development; family violence; substance and behavioral addiction; and mental health. Over the past three decades, she has also worked directly in organizational, clinical, educational and faith settings, with several thousand persons experiencing emotional, substance, relationship and behavioral addictions and "co"-addictions, and other relationship challenges, as well as stress, anxiety and other "disorders." She has also worked with the children of many of the above. Dr. deAngelis is director of the Metaxis Institute based in Corte Madera, California.

Continuity of Life
Seminars and Consultations

by

Dr. Angela deAngelis

Change your life. Change your transitions. Reach beyond unnecessary limits.

Empower yourself to address the large and small challenges, transitions and crises of life—including but not limited to problematic addictions, troubled relationships, difficult and chronic mental and physical health conditions, grief and loss, and death and dying.

Dr. Angela deAngelis is available for consults, treatment programs, workshops, seminars, retreats and trainings. To make appointments and reservations, and to be placed on the Continuity of Life mailing list, email your contact information (including telephone, email address and postal mailing address) to:

DoctorAngela@aol.com
MetaxisInstitute@aol.com

Also check the following websites for information on upcoming events:

DoctorAngela.com
MetaxisInstitute.com

CONTINUITY OF LIFE SERIES

by Dr. Angela deAngelis

Take a new look at healing, health, life and even death. Gain a new perspective on troubles such as diseases, addictions, daily challenges and transitions. Take a journey of the heart, mind and soul into the infinite realm of unbounded hope and possibility, of transformational healing and transcendence.

Begin seeing life and life's adventures as cyclic rather than linear. Discover what must shift for our minds to open to heightened awareness and power. Find out what it is that keeps us from knowing all we can about who we are and what we are capable of within and beyond our physical existence.

This four volume series is written for anyone who has ever encountered an ending or a beginning, a trauma or a transition of any sort, and has a desire to learn what is possible in the evolution of the human consciousness. As you become more aware of this continuity of life, you will begin to initiate yourself into an entirely new energy matrix, always expanding your being.

So, step into the Continuity of Life and walk on . . .

Complete the Series!

VOL.3 - TRANSITION AND SURVIVAL TECHNOLOGIES

$16.95 ISBN-13: 978-1-891824-68-5

VOL.4 - HEALING EARTH IN ALL HER DIMENSIONS

$16.95 ISBN-13: 978-1-891824-69-2

ORDER ONLINE AT WWW.LIGHTTECHNOLOGY.COM

Phone: 928-526-1345 • 800-450-0985 • Fax: 928-714-1132

customersrv@lighttechnology.net

HEALING EARTH IN ALL HER DIMENSIONS $16.95
Softcover, 224pp, ISBN-13: 978-1-891824-69-2

HEALING EARTH IN ALL HER DIMENSIONS:

Personal, Species, and Planetary Healing

by Dr. Angela deAngelis

Explore how interdimensional shifts can be applied to help heal individual bodies, as well as global and ecological systems, to bring about the healing and survival of yourself and the entire human species.

Gain confidence in the truly enduring nature of your consciousness and come to understand how powerful your conscious will, your free will, truly is. With knowledge comes the realization that you can access this eternal and powerful nature before leaving (or traveling to and from) your physical body.

Expand your ability to independently evolve from your physical body. Prepare the way to expand beyond unnecessary limitations to develop new patterns of existence, healing and transition for yourself, your species and your ecosystem.

Chapters Include

- **How to Metamorph**
- **Living the Metamorphosis**
- **Conscious Healing**
- **Conscious Shift Construction**
- **Conscious Metamorphosis**
- **Breaking Addictions to Perceived Reality**
- **Meta-somatic Ailments**
- **Metascending to a New Niche: LEAP Level Seven**
- **Entering Metaterra: How to Access High Metaxis**
- **Conquering Catastrophe Completely**
- **Becoming the Phoenix and Rising**
- **Fueling Freely Willed Ascension**
- **Dying with Grace and Power**

ORDER ONLINE AT WWW.LIGHTTECHNOLOGY.COM
Phone: 928-526-1345 • 800-450-0985 • Fax: 928-714-1132
customersrv@lighttechnology.net

A New Book by
Drunvalo Melchizedek

LIVING IN THE HEART

Includes a CD with Heart Meditation by Drunvalo Melchizedek

$25 with CD
Softcover 120 P.
ISBN 1-891824-43-0

"Long ago we humans used a form of communication and sensing that did not involve the brain in any way; rather, it came from a sacred place within our heart. What good would it do to find this place again in a world where the greatest religion is science and the logic of the mind? Don't I know this world where emotions and feelings are second-class citizens? Yes, I do. But my teachers have asked me to remind you who you really are. You are more than a human being, much more. For within your heart is a place, a sacred place where the world can literally be remade through conscious cocreation. If you give me permission, I will show you what has been shown to me."

- **Beginning with the Mind**
- **Seeing in the Darkness**
- **Learning from Indigenous Tribes**
- **The Sacred Space of the Heart**
- **The Unity of Heaven and Earth**
- **Leaving the Mind and Entering the Heart**
- **The Sacred Space of the Heart Meditation**
- **The Mer-Ka-Ba and the Sacred Space of the Heart**
- **Conscious Cocreation from the Heart Connected to the Mind**

Drunvalo Melchizedek has been studying pure consciousness and human potential for almost forty years. His focus on the rediscovery of the human lightbody, the Mer-Ka-Ba and the way Sacred Geometry is inherent within the lightbody and all of creation is shared through workshops and books as he has brought his vision of the Flower of Life and the Mer-Ka-Ba to the world.

Now his new work, *Living in the Heart*, with the techniques that lead you into the Sacred Space of the Heart, goes even deeper into the possibilities of human potential and the creation process itself. Within these pages, Drunvalo shares his knowledge and tells you exactly how to achieve this ancient state of consciousness so that, finally, what you dream in your heart you can make real in your everyday life; a beautiful, abundant life and ascension into the higher worlds become a natural sequence of living in your heart. Join Drunvalo and be part of the large group of people who have found the joy of living in the space where you and God are one.

Phone: 928-526-1345 or 1-800-450-0985 • Fax: 928-714-1132

THE ANCIENT SECRET OF THE FLOWER OF LIFE
VOLUME 1

Once, all life in the universe knew the Flower of Life as the creation pattern—the geometrical design leading us into and out of physical existence. Then, from a very high state of consciousness, we fell into darkness, the secret hidden for thousands of years, encoded in the cells of all life.

Now we are rising from the darkness and a new dawn is streaming through the windows of perception. This book is one of those windows. Drunvalo Melchizedek presents in text and graphics the Flower of Life Workshop, illuminating the mysteries of how we came to be.

Sacred Geometry is the form beneath our being and points to a divine order in our reality. We can follow that order from the invisible atom to the infinite stars, finding ourselves at each step. The information here is one path, but between the lines and drawings lie the feminine gems of intuitive understanding. You might see them sparkle around some of these provocative ideas:

- Remembering Our Ancient Past
- The Secret of the Flower Unfolds
- The Darker Side of Our Present and Past
- The Geometries of the Human Body
- When Evolution Crashed, and the Christ Grid Arose
- Egypt's Role in the Evolution of Consciousness
- The Significance of Shape and Structure

$25.00 Softcover 228 P.
ISBN 1-891824-17-1

Available from your favorite bookstore or:

LIGHT TECHNOLOGY PUBLISHING
PO Box 3540 • Flagstaff, AZ 86003

Drunvalo Melchizedek's life experience reads like an encyclopedia of breakthroughs in human endeavor. He studied physics and art at the University of California at Berkeley, but he feels that his most important education came after college. In the past 25 years, he has studied with over 70 teachers from all belief systems and religious understandings.

For some time now, he has been bringing his vision to the world through the Flower of Life program and the Mer-Ka-Ba meditation. This teaching encompasses every area of human understanding, explores the development of humankind from ancient civilizations to the present time and offers clarity regarding the world's state of consciousness and what is needed for a smooth and easy transition into the 21st century.

Phone: 928-526-1345 or 1-800-450-0985 • Fax: 928-714-1132

New From Light Technology!

THE GENTLE WAY

A SELF-HELP GUIDE FOR THOSE WHO BELIEVE IN ANGELS

Let me explain what I believe you'll achieve from reading this self-help book:

This book will put you back in touch with your guardian angel or strengthen and expand the connection that perhaps you already have. It will strengthen your spiritual beliefs. You will have more fun and less stress in your life. You will greatly lower the "fear factor" in everyday living. In lowering the fear factor, this book will give you the confidence that you can travel in safety wherever you go, whether it is to work and back home, to the store, across the country or around the world. It will assist you in achieving whatever goals you have set for yourself in your life. This book will assist in finding just the right job for you. It will even help you find that special person to share your life. It will assist you in handling those major challenges we all experience in life. This book will even inspire you to learn more about our world and universe. How can I promise all these benefits? It's because I have been using these concepts for over ten years, and I can report these successes from *direct knowledge and experience*. But this is a self-help guide, so that means it requires active participation on your part. What you are going to read in this book is *unique information* that you have *never seen before!* This book is for all faiths and beliefs with the only requirement being a basic belief in angels.

—Tom T. Moore

CHAPTER TITLES:

- ANGELS
- HOW I BEGAN
- EASY STEPS
- HOME LIFE
- THE CORPORATE ENVIRONMENT
- SMALL BUSINESSES
- POLITICS
- TRAVEL
- BINGO, CASINOS AND CARD GAMES
- REQUESTING BENEVOLENT OUTCOMES IN DANGEROUS PLACES
- THE RADIANT EFFECT
- LIVING PRAYERS
- "I HOPE" REQUESTS

$14.95 Softcover
ISBN 1-891824-60-0

Visit our online bookstore: www.lighttechnology.com

TOOLS FOR TRANSFORMATION

VYWAMUS channeled by Janet McClure

PRELUDE TO ASCENSION
Tools for Transformation

Janet McClure channeling Djwhal Khul, Vywamus & others

Your four bodies, the Tibetan Lessons series, the Twelve Rays, the Cosmic Walk-in and others. All previously unpublished channelings by Janet McClure.

$29.95, SOFTCOVER 850 P. • ISBN 0-929385-54-3

THE SOURCE ADVENTURE

Life is discovery, and this book is a journey of discovery "to learn, to grow, to recognize the opportunities—to be aware." It asks the big question, "Why are you here?" and leads the reader to examine the most significant questions of a lifetime.

$11.95, SOFTCOVER 157 P. • ISBN 0-929385-06-3

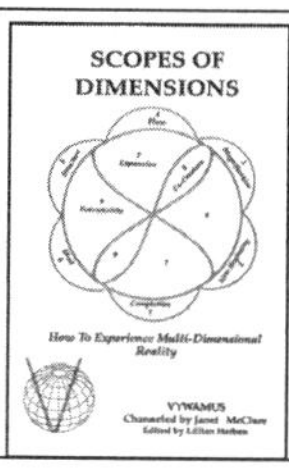

SCOPES OF DIMENSIONS

Vywamus explains the process of exploring and experiencing the dimensions. He teaches an integrated way to utilize the combined strengths of each dimension. It is a how-to guidebook for living in the multidimensional reality that is our true evolutionary path.

$11.95, SOFTCOVER 176 P. • ISBN 0-929385-09-8

AHA! THE REALIZATION BOOK
(with Lillian Harben)

If you are mirroring your life in a way that is not desirable, this book can help you locate murky areas and make them "suddenly . . . crystal clear." Readers will discover an exciting step by step path to changing and evolving their lives.

$11.95, SOFTCOVER 120 P. • ISBN 0-929385-14-4

SANAT KUMARA
Training a Planetary Logos

How was the beauty of this world created? The answer is in the story of Earth's Logos, the great being Sanat Kumara. It is a journey through his eyes as he learns the real-life lessons of training along the path of mastery.

$11.95, SOFTCOVER 179 P. • ISBN 0-929385-17-9

LIGHT TECHNIQUES
That Trigger Transformation

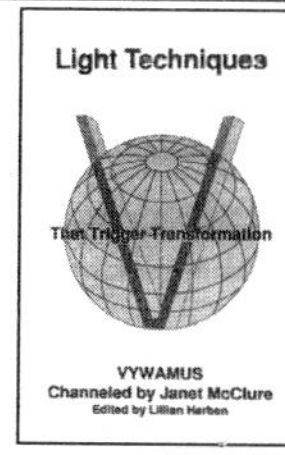

Expanding the heart center, launching your light, releasing the destructive focus, weaving a garment of light, light alignment and more, this book is a wonderfully effective tool for using light to transcend. Beautiful guidance!

$11.95, SOFTCOVER 145 P. • ISBN 0-929385-00-4

Phone: 928-526-1345 or 1-800-450-0985 • Fax: 928-714-1132